SHEVOLUTION

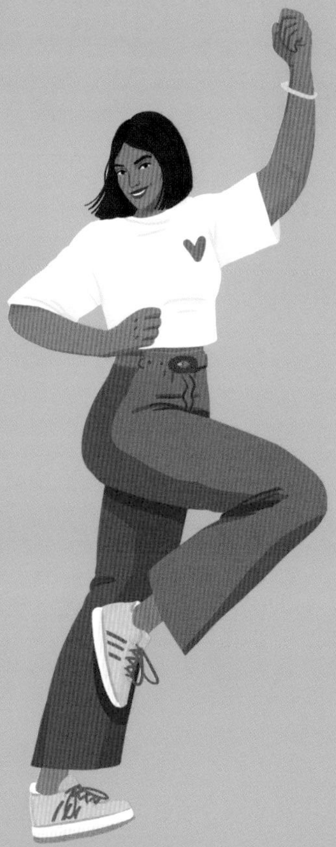

Published in the UK, 2025
Scholastic, Bosworth Avenue, Warwick, CV34 6XZ
Scholastic Ireland, 89E Lagan Road, Dublin Industrial Estate, Glasnevin, Dublin, D11 HP5F

ISBN 978 0702 33382 8

A CIP catalogue record for this book is available from the British Library.

Printed in UK by Bell & Bain Ltd, Glasgow
Paper made from wood grown in sustainable forests and other controlled sources.

1 3 5 7 9 10 8 6 4 2

www.scholastic.co.uk

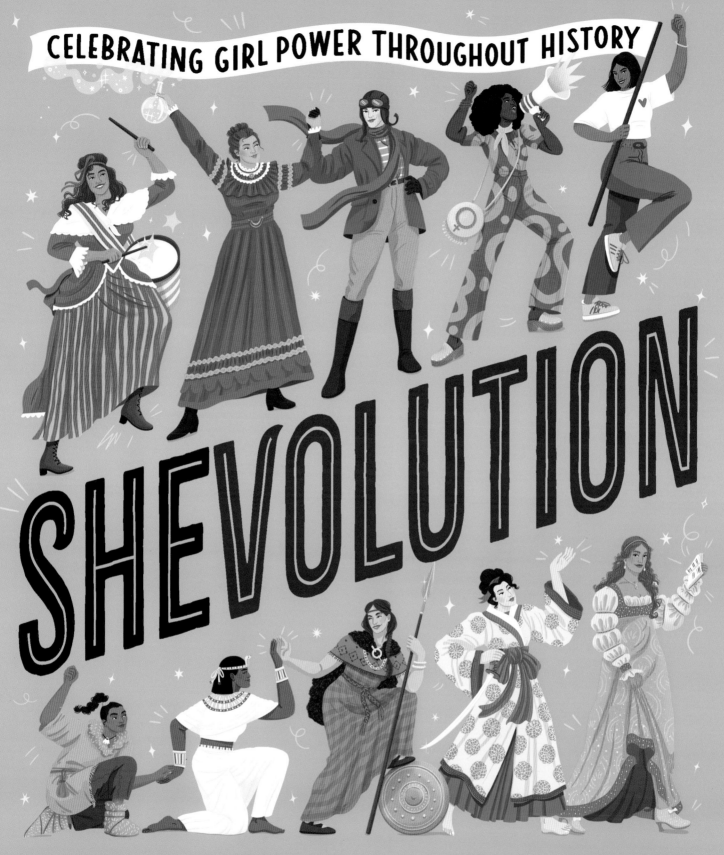

CELEBRATING GIRL POWER THROUGHOUT HISTORY

SHEVOLUTION

WRITTEN BY
LOU TRELEAVEN

ILLUSTRATED BY
PETRA BRAUN

SCHOLASTIC

CONTENTS

IN THE BEGINNING 7

WHERE IS EVERYONE? 8

PRINCESS, PRIESTESS, POET 10

EQUALITY CALLS 13

AN IRON WILL 14

THE POWER OF WRITING 16

PLOTS AND PLANS 18

DARK TIMES 20

NOT SO MANY CHOICES 23

WISE ADVICE 24

FORMIDABLE DAYS FOR FORMIDABLE WOMEN 26

THE ORIGINAL INFLUENCERS 28

STRANGE OPINIONS 30

THE WITCHING HOUR 32

TWO QUEENS 34

THE JOSEON KINGDOM 37

REVOLUTIONARY REBELS 38

FACTORY GIRLS 40

THE ARMY OF THE AGOJIE 42

SCIENCE AGAINST THE ODDS 44

VICTORIA AND THE VICTORIANS 46

WOMEN AND SLAVERY **48**

SUBVERSIVE SISTERS **51**

THE STORY OF VOTES FOR WOMEN **52**

FIGHTING FOR THE VOTE **54**

DARING TO DISCOVER **56**

THE WAR TO END ALL WARS **58**

DANGEROUS NURSING **60**

AN UNCERTAIN TIME **62**

BREAKING AWAY **64**

SPIES AND SACRIFICES **66**

THE WOMEN OF BLETCHLEY **68**

PERSECUTION **71**

THE 'PERFECT' HOUSEWIFE **72**

THE CIVIL RIGHTS MOVEMENT **74**

EMPOWERED VOICES **76**

TECH TITANS **78**

WAR AND PEACE **80**

AN AGE OF EXTREMES **82**

BEGINNINGS AND ENDINGS **84**

NEW MILLENNIUM, NEW CHALLENGES **87**

PROTESTS AND THE PLANET **88**

SPRINTING AHEAD **90**

EVE'S LEGACY **92**

GLOSSARY **94**

INDEX **96**

IN THE BEGINNING

There is a beginning to every story and this story begins with one woman. Before there was you – or your sister – there was Eve. At the start of our *Shevolution*, before there were queens ruling countries or girls going to school, there was Eve: a powerful, enterprising, strong-willed survivor. She could have had any name, but whatever her name was, she is our worldwide common ancestor. Mother to us all. Our shared relative and the origin of our *Shevolution*.

Eve might have lived around 200,000 years ago, but she still would have looked like us. She would have talked and laughed with her friends like us, marvelled at sunsets, gazed at the Moon and fallen in love like us. But her life would have been very, very different to ours. Instead of sleeping in a nice warm bed, she would have curled up under the stars. Instead of popping into a shop when she was hungry, she would have had to hunt for meat and gather fruit, nuts and roots.

Scientists call this woman Eve because in the Jewish, Christian and Islamic religions, Eve was the first woman.

You might be wondering how in the world we know that everyone alive today is related to one woman. Surely that's impossible? The answer is in our DNA – this special instruction code that tells your body how to breathe, grow, live and learn; that tells you how much you look like the other members of your family, even sometimes how much you behave like them.

Inside our cells is a very special type of DNA – mitochondrial DNA – which is only passed on from our mothers. This means that scientists can use this DNA to trace back an unbroken chain from every woman and girl all the way back to one: Eve.

Sometimes the person we think of as 'Eve' will change. As family lines end, the most common ancestor to us all will switch to another woman.

Right now, the person we think of as Eve lived in Southern Africa in the Stone Age. She would have had a family and a community and no idea that one day, eight billion people would be related to her.

WHERE IS EVERYONE?

Eight billion would have been an unimaginable number to Eve. Her life – and the lives of every modern human at that point in time – would have been lived in Africa. There may have only been 50,000 people like her in existence and almost certainly no more than a million. At this stage, humans had been using stone tools for around 2.4 million years, giving us the 'Stone Age' name, and Eve's family would have picked up new skills as they grew, just like you. They were pretty good at it, too.

At the beginning of the Stone Age, as humans got to grips with their new stone tools, a Stone-Age woman might be wrapped in animal skins, living in a cave eating nuts and berries, and – if she was lucky – the occasional small creature, before moving on to a new location. By the end of the Stone Age, nearly three million years later, she'd be more likely to be living in a clay hut, cooking freshly speared deer over a fire, with a nice broth boiling away in a fancy homemade pot. She would also have had a stylish-for-the-time handsewn outfit, thanks to the invention of the needle.

Before the idea of farming cropped up around 10,000 years ago, people lived by either hunting or gathering food. Many people imagine that it would have been the men who charged off with spears to hunt for animals

to kill and eat, while the women stayed near the cave looking after the children and prepping a side salad from their finds on a recent foraging trip. But guess what? They're wrong. Recently, historians looking at Stone-Age graves have discovered new evidence: female skeletons buried with valuable spears, just like male hunters. And doesn't that make sense? With so few people and every one of them important for the survival of the group, everyone would have done whatever was necessary to eat and to live. Of course! Being smaller and lighter, women would have been good at creeping up on their prey – even if they had a baby strapped to them at the time. Stone-Age women were multi-skilled survival specialists.

Life wasn't only hunting, gathering and heading back to the family cave though. Just like you, people would have had downtime, but without a games console or the internet, Stone-Age leisure time would have been rather different to yours. With no social media to record your every move, what could you do to let people know about your life? Paint. Paint the cave, in fact. Cave-dwelling people left many beautiful clues to their existence, painting animals and people on the walls. You can even see the shapes of their hands, as they used them as stencils, painting around them to create patterns and prints, even holding pigment in their mouths to 'spray paint' over them. Recent studies of these hand stencils have revealed something wonderful: many are female, which makes it likely that the stunning paintings they have been found next to are by female artists, too.

A hundred thousand years after Eve was keeping herself busy with stone tools, hunting and gathering her food, and decorating her cave with her exploits, her descendants began to travel. They began to leave Africa and gradually started the spread of humankind around the world.

PRINCESS, PRIESTESS, POET

✦★✦★✦✦★✦★✦✦★✦★✦✦★✦★✦✦★✦★✦✦★✦★✦✦★✦★✦✦★✦★✦✦★✦

Once people started to move beyond their original home in Africa, developments for Eve's later descendants happened at different times in different locations – not surprising since there was no way then to let people far away know what you'd discovered. And discover they did! People began to dig for copper around ten thousand years ago in what would eventually be Iraq. Later, when tin was discovered, people found that together they made a harder metal: bronze. And so the Bronze Age began, initially here and there until the knowledge spread or was discovered all over. That wasn't the only new development. People also started to farm, planting crops and keeping animals penned in and protected from wild predators so they could use them for food. Villages, towns and even cities began to spring up; eventually whole nations were created. Ancient burials found in Spain show women buried with men in lavish, expensive tombs situated under important buildings, meaning they both would have held powerful positions. Men and women also dressed the same in skirts or shifts, and both carried daggers. Bronze-Age women could be powerful queens, priestesses or warriors. Some were even all three...

How do you tell a male skeleton from a female? You might think they're all the same, but actually a woman's skeleton looks different to a man's. Because women are able to give birth, their pelvises – the bony frames that keep our legs attached to us – are wider.

In an age where there was still so much to be discovered and understood, people believed in many different things. The world was a great mystery, and perhaps belief in a variety of gods helped people find a way to understand the mystery. Some of these gods were female and were served by female priestesses. If you were a priestess, you would usually live at the temple dedicated to your goddess. Your job would be to offer gifts of things like food and clothing, and even animal sacrifices. You could also perform marriages and help people who had illnesses or injuries. Another of your jobs would have been to predict the future. No need for a crystal ball though. All you had to do was look through the guts of a freshly killed animal and you would find a way to work out what the gods wanted. You could also interpret dreams, which were seen as messages sent from the gods. It was probably a difficult job, especially if you were telling someone something they did not want to hear.

Priestesses also had the chance to be creative and write their own songs and hymns. **ENHEDUANNA** of Mesopotamia (where Iraq, Syria and Turkey are today) wrote many hymns to the goddess Inanna. They were so popular that they were inscribed on stone tablets and can still be read today. Before Enheduanna's time, it wasn't usual for authors to put their names to their writing. But this talented priestess wrote about herself in her songs and how wonderful it felt to create art. You could say she was the first celebrity author.

Priestesses were usually from ruling families so they would quite often be rulers themselves as well. Enheduanna was one such priestess. Her father was Sargon the Great of Akkad. People who lived in Akkad worshipped a fierce goddess called Ishtar, while in nearby Sumeria the people worshipped the more gentle goddess Inanna. When Sargon the Great conquered Sumeria, Enheduanna helped him by writing songs that merged the two goddesses, so that eventually people started thinking of them as one and the same. Having this common belief made it easier for Sargon to rule his people.

EQUALITY CALLS

In ancient Egypt, a woman had more freedom and rights than in some countries today. She was free to find a career, to fall in – and out of – love, to fight and to lead. The Egyptians believed in *ma'at* or balance in all things. There were even god and goddess couples. Isis ruled over humanity together with her husband Osiris and gave the gift of equality between men and women to her people. Well, almost. Men were the heads of their households, but women could choose who to marry, travel where they wanted, hold important jobs and had equal legal rights, unlike women of other societies at the time, such as the ancient Greeks.

It's said that a Greek woman named **AGNODICE** wanted to be a doctor, but she wasn't allowed to train in her own country because of her sex. Agnodice was so determined to follow her dream that she travelled to Egypt to become a doctor there. She then returned home to work, but it still wasn't easy. Agnodice had to disguise herself as a man in order to work as a doctor in her own country.

If you were a woman in ancient Egypt and wanted to get one of the more desirable jobs, the starting point was to become a scribe – someone who recorded events and finances, and kept things organized, all using hieroglyphs written in ink on papyrus. To become a scribe meant years of study, but once qualified you could become a priest, a teacher or a doctor.

If you were a woman who didn't have the money to study to become a scribe or you weren't born into the right family, you could do a more manual job such as weaver, baker, cook, brewer, launderer or sandal-maker. The wealthier classes employed people or forced enslaved people to work for them.

To bag the very top job in Egypt, the only way was to become a wife of the pharaoh, or ruler, and work your way up to being the top wife: the queen. The queen would help her husband govern and stand in for him if he was travelling or away at war.

HATSHEPSUT was the most powerful queen of ancient Egypt. She even ruled on her own as pharaoh when her husband died. During her reign, she organized adventurous trading expeditions, fought alongside her soldiers in battle and had many impressive buildings erected. The most famous were four huge obelisks inscribed with writing glorifying the gods – and herself, of course.

As an ancient-Egyptian woman, you were free to marry who you wanted – but you had to choose wisely. Your marriage would last into the afterlife and for all eternity. If things went wrong, though, you could get divorced. Unlike in some time periods and countries, even today, divorce was not seen as shameful, and the woman could keep the family home and her children. However, the hope was for a happy union, and the rights that women and girls were afforded gave them much greater power to achieve their own happiness.

BASTET was the daughter of the Sun god and a popular goddess for many ancient-Egyptian women. Her special concerns were the home, family, childbirth and women's secrets. Women would make offerings to her or carry amulets in her form in the hope of getting her help. Because she took the form of a cat, cats in ancient Egypt were treated with great admiration and respect. They still demand this same treatment today.

AN IRON WILL

As the *Shevolution* continued – although at a very different pace in different places – there was another leap forward for the descendants of Eve. People worked out how to extract iron from rock and use it to make steel. This new material meant that weapons and tools became much stronger. Farming improved, it was now possible to build larger structures and war became ever more deadly. The Iron Age had begun, and Iron-Age women were ready for it.

What were people in the Iron Age like? How different were their lives to yours? When men died in Iron-Age Britain, they were usually buried with a sword and a shield. Iron-Age women were buried with a brooch and a mirror. But an ancient grave on Bryher – an island in the Scilly Isles – had scientists puzzled for a long time. The grave contained a sword and a shield ... and a brooch and a mirror. Was this a man or a woman? All that was left of the body were a few small pieces of bone and teeth, so the shape wasn't obvious, and the remains were too decayed to test for DNA. But then things changed. Scientists discovered that a person's sex can be found out through their tooth enamel. The teeth were examined, and the ancient body was discovered to be female. Mirrors are thought to have been used in battle for signalling and also for communicating with the gods, so the items left in the grave point to the woman being a warrior or powerful leader. And ancient sites are still unlocking secrets about the lives of mighty Iron-Age women.

If you wanted something to last for thousands of years, you wouldn't think of putting it in a bog, but that's exactly what happened to some Iron-Age bodies. Bogs and swamps can preserve bodies because they prevent oxygen from causing decay. They are also full of a chemical called tannin, which preserves soft body tissue and even clothing.

An Iron-Age woman was dug up from a bog in Huldremose, Denmark, and scientists were able to discover some amazing things about her, including that her last meal was rye, seeds and some sort of meat. They also found that she had once broken her leg, but it had healed, her right arm was almost severed, she was around 40 years old – quite elderly for the Iron Age! – and she lived her life over 2,200 years ago.

She wore a checked woollen skirt that was once blue, a scarf that used to be bright red and two sheepskin capes.

She had some precious keepsakes sewn into her clothing: an old horn comb, a blue hairband and a leather cord.

Bogs were used to making offerings to the gods and to sacrifice animals. Was the woman a human sacrifice, or was her death a sad accident? Was her arm injured before or after death? Her ultimate secrets will never be known, but at least now she will be remembered by history.

The Celts of Ireland worshipped many gods in the Iron Age, but their goddesses were just as important.

THE POWER OF WRITING

The age of antiquity – the Classical Era – began around two and a half thousand years ago. This was when people started to record their own history and we can know and understand much more about the lives of women and girls in our *Shevolution*. At this time, huge empires expanded across continents and Greek and Roman influences were everywhere: from politics and law to architecture, language and art. A new age was coming.

Away from Europe, the Persian empire grew across Western Asia from ancient Iran and was the first empire we know of to accept the different faiths and languages of its subjects, instead of trying to change them. Persian women also had more rights and freedoms than women would 2,000 years later in Victorian England: they could own lands and estates, supervise workers and travel freely for business or pleasure. Some even fought in the Persian army alongside men. Women received equal pay, and actually got more pay if they were pregnant. How do we know all this? We can read the records. Inscribed tablets found in the ruins of the city of Persepolis show travel expenses being paid to women from royal funds. These freedoms stopped, however, when the Persian empire finally fell, conquered by armies from the nearby Arabian empire.

Of all the mighty women in Persia, **IRDABAMA** was probably the most powerful. A trader and merchant, she had nearly 500 people working for her, and owned vineyards and farms in Babylonia, Egypt, Media and Syria. But Irdabama didn't just sit back and let the money roll in. She spent a lot of time travelling and making sure everything was running smoothly. As a result, Irdabama was one of the richest women of her time.

Unlike in Persia, a woman's life over in ancient Greece was very restricted. While men could go about freely, as a woman you were expected to stay inside your home or courtyard. If you really had to, you could visit a neighbour and attend public events, so you would probably be desperate for the next wedding, funeral or religious ceremony to be held. Your job was to raise the children, cook and sew. If you lived on a farm, you might help with the harvesting. Apart from that there were no career options for women. As an ancient-Greek girl you might be taught some basic lessons at home, but your main task was to learn how to run a household. Once you reached your teenage years, you were married off and had to run your own home.

There was one role for a Greek woman that did give her power. And it was a role unlike any other. The oracle, or Pythia, was a special priestess who predicted the future. If you wanted to know how your latest war might end, you would ask the oracle. If you wanted to get some guidance on the fate of your empire, you'd ask the oracle. It can't have been easy to get this job – and the privilege that came with it – although it's not entirely known what the selection process would have been like.

It is known that you would be a woman over 50 and would have to live away from your family at the temple of Apollo in Delphi, and – just a few times a year – you would have to descend to the lower level of the temple and enter an altered state, so that you could make your predictions. It's possible that there, deep underground, gases released from the earth below helped to make the oracle reach that state. Whatever you said during the ceremony was recorded and interpreted by others and was believed to be advice from Apollo himself. You would do this until the end of your life, at which point the next oracle would be chosen. The oracles are a rare example of Greek women in ancient times having the power to influence society.

Enslavement was common in Greece during this time, and even an average home would have three or four slaves living and working in it. They might be captured prisoners or born into slavery.

An enslaved woman had even fewer rights than a free one, and her quality of life depended entirely on her enslaver.

PLOTS AND PLANS

While the women chosen to make predictions at Apollo's temple in Delphi were still going about their work, the Romans began to expand their empire. At one point Roman territories became so vast that one in four people on the planet were Roman citizens. You may already know that the Romans are famous for introducing the world to plumbing, straight roads, the modern calendar, a single currency, spas, underfloor heating and even fast food (perfect for hungry Roman soldiers on the move), but you may not have heard much about the lives of Roman women. Despite being so advanced in so many ways, the ancient Romans, much like the ancient Greeks, valued women as wives and mothers. And like ancient-Greek women, Roman women were expected to concentrate on running the home. You could have a job, but it was rare, and power would be out of your reach.

The only way you could have a big influence on the world stage was to marry a leader – or give birth to one...

Female members of Emperor Augustus's family had very colourful lives, but their exploits often put them in danger. The emperor's only biological child, **JULIA THE ELDER**, did not behave as her father wished. To help his political schemes, Augustus chose a husband for Julia – not once, but three times. Julia's first two husbands died and the third left her. Julia decided to form her own relationships instead, but Augustus was so angry with her behaviour that he had her banished to an island in 2 BCE.

Julia's daughter, **AGRIPPINA THE ELDER**, was lucky enough to have a happy marriage and a large family – until her husband died in mysterious circumstances. Boldly she accused the next emperor, Tiberius, of poisoning him. When Tiberius refused her request for a grand public funeral, she brought her husband's ashes home to Rome herself and paraded with them down the streets to Augustus's royal tomb, accompanied by crowds of mourners. By disobeying the emperor in this way she was basically accusing him of murder and Tiberius never forgave her. His revenge was long and slow. He executed one of her sons, and a second son died of hunger in exile. Agrippina the Elder was also exiled to an island, where she starved to death in 33 CE.

Julia's granddaughter, **AGRIPPINA THE YOUNGER**, was just as fiery a character as her mother and grandmother. Her aim was to put her son, Nero, on the throne, so she married Emperor Claudius and persuaded him to make Nero his heir. She then, so the rumour goes, cooked up a poisonous mushroom supper to finish him off in the year 54 CE. Agrippina was also rumoured to have killed her first husband and to have plotted to kill her brother so she had a slightly murderous history. The small problem remained of Claudius already having a son of his own ready to be the emperor, but Nero helped out by murdering his stepbrother and taking the throne. Agrippina had succeeded in her ambition. But, as teenagers sometimes do, Nero soon got tired of having an interfering mother around and, after a number of failed attempts, finally managed to have her assassinated in 59 CE.

Agrippina had brought her son up to be as ruthless and deadly as herself.

Julia the Elder

Agrippina the younger

Agrippina the Elder

DARK TIMES

Sixteen hundred years ago, as the mighty Roman empire fell, culture and science began to take a back seat. Warring tribes, invasions and religious differences created division among the now millions of people on Earth. The early Middle Ages – the Dark Ages – saw superstition, strict hierarchy and the power of the church take over. In Europe, there was a societal place for everyone. This 'feudal' system placed the monarch at the top of the heap with their lords directly below them, followed by knights, then farmers and merchants, with lowly peasants beneath them all. Serfs – the lowest of the low – were firmly at the bottom, lower even than peasants. At every level, women and girls were considered 'less than' and 'possessions' of their husbands or fathers. Even rich women were treated as objects to be fought over, won and lost, and their education was deliberately limited. The most powerful women were usually widows who were able to take over their husband's affairs and businesses, but even then a male relative might still be on hand to tell them what to do.

A woman named **CHRISTINE DE PIZAN** was one of the rare medieval women to have a good education. And her education was thanks to having access to a library. It was not just any old library, either. Christine was the daughter of the royal astrologer for Charles V of France and lived at court where she had access to the kind of education – and reading material – usually reserved for boys. A few years into her young marriage, Christine's husband died, leaving her with three children and the need to make a living. And so she wrote. At first she worked as a scribe – writing for other people – but then she began to write her own ideas.

And they were brilliant!

She wrote letters, essays and books including *The Book of the City of Ladies* in 1405 which imagined a town that was run and lived in only by women. Her point was that if women are given equal rights they can contribute equally to society.

The medieval era also brought with it the Black Death, which was a horrific plague that swept across the Islamic world and Europe in the 14th century. Starting with egg-sized swellings in the armpits or groin, the Black Death caused fever, sickness and diarrhoea, and, for one in three people, a speedy and painful death. The population shrank and, for decades afterwards, many women who had been widowed went on to run their husbands' businesses and make important decisions. But, as the population regrew, these freedoms and new opportunities were lost again.

Back in the Middle Ages you would not have been able to choose your husband. Marriages were arranged by parents and were used to boost the family's finances or place in society. As a girl in medieval Europe you could be married from the age of 12 and would join your husband's family with a big bag of cash (if they were lucky) called a dowry. If you had any possessions or land of your own, that would go to your husband, too. Before the wedding, a notice would be put on the church door in case anyone wanted to object. Reasons for not being able to marry included: being too closely related, trying to get married on a feast day, being a monk or nun, or the priest being a murderer.

Religions and beliefs changed a lot in the Middle Ages. Before this era, most people worshipped pagan gods representing things like the Sun and Moon, or ideas such as love, war or nature. The spread of organized religions like Christianity and Islam across Europe and Western Asia meant that their powerful leaders became bigger influences. The idea that women should stay in the role of dutiful homemaker won out and those who stood out for being 'different' were viewed with suspicion, violence or even a death sentence for being a 'witch'.

NOT SO MANY CHOICES

Just like in ancient Rome, one of the few ways women in medieval times could wield any sort of power or influence was through marriage to a high-status man. A woman named **ELEANOR OF AQUITAINE** did just that – not just once, but twice.

Eleanor's father was the super-rich Duke of Aquitaine in France. When her father and brother died, Eleanor became a very wealthy woman. This may have been why she was married off to the heir to the French throne in 1137, who would later become King Louis VII. The couple did not get on well, but – luckily, being the king – Louis was able to have their marriage annulled in 1152. Eleanor then got hitched to Henry Plantagenet, the future king of England, that same year. That marriage didn't go too well either … to say the least. Eleanor even plotted to kill her husband and Henry had her imprisoned. After Henry's death in 1189, Eleanor's son, Richard, became king and released her. An experienced ruler now in her sixties, Eleanor helped to run England and France, stood in for King Richard when he was abroad, and returned the favour by helping to get him released when he was taken prisoner. When Richard died, Eleanor retired from court life but was still very involved in affairs in her homeland of Aquitaine until her death in 1204. She was buried next to Henry – something probably neither of them would have wanted.

Of course, not many women had the option of becoming a queen.

And, since surgeon, director, judge, prime minister and champion athlete were all firmly off the careers table, you'd have to look to what is now a more unusual alternative in order to avoid marrying and living under the control of a husband – becoming a nun. The Benedictines were a popular order of Christian nuns, but new orders such as the Poor Clares began to appear in the Middle Ages and opened up new opportunities for girls and their families. It might not sound terribly appealing, and life as a nun could be harsh – you had to live very simply by strict rules and spend your life praying and serving your community – but you would be independent from your family and the demands of society. You might also be able to read books and educate yourself. A standout nun at the time was the almost superhumanly clever Hildegard of Bingen. She studied philosophy, music composition, medicine, literature, biology and cosmology, and made advances in science as well as being famous for her religious visions and her music.

For women like Hildegard, convents could provide the space and time to pursue their own interests away from the world.

WISE ADVICE

In the Middle Ages, whether you were a nun or a queen or a young girl waiting to see which way life would go, if you got sick, there were no doctors' surgeries to go to for help. Instead, you might seek out the village wise woman. She would rummage through her herbs and natural remedies for the right cure and might give you a charm or even perform a 'spell' to help make you feel better. These homespun remedies sound a bit haphazard today, but the skills and traditions were based on knowledge gathered over many years and handed down from mother to daughter. Women were also much more familiar than men with handling the human body, as they helped each other give birth and raise their children.

Later on, as universities were founded and men began to train formally in medicine, healing became a male profession, and female healers could be punished for not being qualified. By the end of the Middle Ages, women who muttered spells and had unnatural knowledge of plants were seen as working for the devil and could be accused of witchcraft. Only helping with childbirth was still seen as a woman's job, and the village midwife remained on hand to ensure the *Shevolution* would continue.

There is an amazing record of advice shared between a group of wise women in Belgium in the 1400s called the Distaff Gospels. They show how healing, tradition and superstition were entwined, resulting in some creative remedies...

To protect yourself from nine different diseases, ride a bear for nine paces.

Stay away from swords while pregnant. If you do get too near a sword, ask the sword-bearer to tap you on the top of the head with the flat of the sword. You'll give birth to an extra-brave baby!

To avoid tremors, don't eat a cat's head.

And finally, you won't get back pain if you never wipe your bottom with a leaf!

For many illnesses there was no hope of a cure and, unlike you, a child in the Middle Ages was not invited to be vaccinated against them. Riding a bear would do absolutely no good against measles or chickenpox, so a Middle Ages childhood was a particularly dangerous one. Girls who survived to become adults then faced another deadly danger: giving birth. Labour pains were thought

to be God's punishment for human sin (fortunately untrue) and, with no painkillers, no medical help and no hygiene, it was a risky experience. But never fear, you could always have worn a birthing girdle: a piece of parchment with special prayers on it that would be strapped around your waist. It would not have done anything for the pain, but may have done something to ease anxiety at least.

FORMIDABLE DAYS FOR FORMIDABLE WOMEN

You might wonder if medieval times might have been a bit better for women outside Europe. Anything is possible ... but ... no. Take medieval Japan. As a child you obeyed your father, then when you grew up you obeyed your husband. If your husband died, you obeyed your son. Women even ate separately from men. So life for women born in medieval Japan was not so very different to the lives of women in Europe. But it wasn't all bad and – if you were lucky enough to be born into the right family – you might find some exciting opportunities.

POETIC IMMORTAL

If you were born a noblewoman you would have had a rare possession: leisure time. Some noblewomen used this luxury to write and create art. Some outstanding female poets nurtured their skills and, of the 36 poets declared 'Poetic Immortals' in an 11th-century Japanese poetry anthology, five were women. **IZUMI SHIKIBU** was a famous poet known as 'the Floating Lady'. She specialized in poems of love and longing and lived at the emperor's court. She was fairly low in rank, which meant she could observe the comings and goings and the court gossip without too much notice. She wrote a diary-style account of court life, alternating entries with her poems. Her vivid, wistful creations are still admired today.

FEARLESS WARRIOR

The samurai were the aristocratic warrior class in Japan. If you were born into this class you were trained to fight. It was mostly men who fought in battle, but women also carried weapons and were expected to defend their homes, children and crops. They were even presented with a knife on their wedding day. However there are also records of female samurai fighting in wars alongside men. **TOMOE GOZEN** was the most renowned. By all accounts she was a fearless commander, and was described in an epic poem of the time as 'a match for a thousand warriors'.

A CLAWED ATTACK

Kunoichi were female ninjas or shinobi – a type of secret warrior, sent to spy on and sometimes assassinate members of the samurai. They were feared even more than the male ninjas because no one suspected these 'innocent-looking' women – until they slipped on their Neko-te. These were claws up to 7.5 centimetres (3 inches) in length that the kunoichi used to attack their enemies. Poison could be added to the tips for maximum impact.

THE ARTFUL ASSASSIN

Gei means art, and geisha were highly trained entertainers who sang, danced, played music and acted as gracious hosts. But their visits could have a more deadly purpose: occasionally they were asked to act as spies and sometimes even assassins.

DOWN ON THE FARM

Exciting opportunities weren't likely to come your way if you were born into a lower-class family. Rather than dramatic assassin work, you'd be more likely to find work on a nearby farm. Not for you a life of leisurely poetry-writing – digging, planting, weeding and harvesting would be the order of the day, every day.

A SERVING OF SAMURAI

If farming wasn't the role for you, there were other opportunities, but don't get your hopes up too soon. In medieval times there were very few labour-saving devices. No vacuum cleaners or fridge-freezers here to move our *Shevolution* along (and the microwave and air fryer were even further off the horizon). If a job needed doing, you'd either have to do it yourself or – if you were of a higher class – get one of your servants to do it. Working for the senior samurai class was seen as the most desirable position for lower-class women who hadn't gone down the farming route.

THE MONEY COUNTERS

If you were a member of a merchant family, you might be taught to read and write as a child so that you could be put in charge of the business accounts. Your family could become quite wealthy in this area, but you'd actually be seen as part of one of the lowest classes of society. This was because merchants sold things that others had made rather than having the skill to make goods themselves. In medieval Japan, there was greater respect given to the craft than to the selling.

Lucrezia

THE ORIGINAL INFLUENCERS

Back in Europe, after the dark and turbulent times of the Middle Ages, culture, art, literature and science began to flourish once more. It was a rebirth of all these things and, because the Italian states were at the heart of this rebirth, this time is known as the Renaissance. Of course, women's lives were still very much limited and under the control of their fathers and then their husbands. And, of course, being born into a wealthy family could help you be more independent, but you were also more likely to be forced into a tactical marriage to benefit your family rather than finding someone you actually liked. But, despite the limitations they faced, some Italian women still found a way to become forces to be reckoned with.

LUCREZIA BORGIA, the daughter of a cardinal who would become pope, was born into the notorious – and criminal – Borgia family. She was highly educated and fluent in many languages, but used like a chess piece by her father, so that he could grab more political power. He married Lucrezia off three times, getting her divorced when he no longer needed the family connection.

Luckily, Lucrezia's third marriage was a happier one than her first and second and, as Duchess of Ferrara, she became an influential woman in society, leading an artistic community and skilfully administering the Ferrara estate. When her father died she could finally live her own life, free from the Borgia family's power games. Lucrezia also had a famous sister-in-law, Isabella d'Este...

Going to school might not always feel like fun – especially on a gloomy Monday morning – but can you imagine if going to school wasn't even an option, let alone a right? Getting an education wasn't on the cards for children from lower-income families, and even people with money didn't bother educating boys and girls equally. A Renaissance girl from a wealthy family might learn languages, the classics and some maths along with music, dance and art, but she wouldn't learn nearly as much as her brothers. Enter **ISABELLA D'ESTE**. She certainly learned all these things, but her parents were different. They believed in educating their children equally. By the time she was 16, Isabella had become

28

Isabella

Sofonisba

a real scholar, as well as a talented musician and dancer, and was able to hold her own in conversations with ambassadors and artists alike. When her husband, the Marquis of Mantua, was away at war, Isabella ruled their people herself, improving the textile-based economy and promoting art and culture. With her money she helped legendary Renaissance artists such as Leonardo da Vinci and Michelangelo. She travelled all over Italy and wrote many letters about her experiences, so many that 12,000 of them still survive today. She also bought land and sheltered thousands of refugees when Rome was invaded in 1527.

Skilled in many areas, she was a true Renaissance woman of power.

Even though there were many incredible artists in Italy in this time, it was a real challenge for a woman to become one herself. Most students studied under experienced artists first, and those artists were men.

They weren't likely to take on a female apprentice. The scandal! Another barrier for female artists was the need to study anatomy to understand how to draw the human body accurately. Was there any chance of girls going to an anatomy lesson? Absolutely not. Despite this, some exceptional female artists broke through these barriers and managed to make a name for themselves.

SOFONISBA ANGUISSOLA was Italian-born but became court painter for the king of Spain due to her astounding artistic talents. The legendary Michelangelo even gave her advice on her paintings and drawings. She is known for her self-portraits, which fewer people painted at the time, and for her pictures of the female members of her family who posed for her. Sofonisba's paintings are now on display in galleries around the world.

STRANGE OPINIONS

Just like today, not everyone in history was able to become an influencer, but many people's minds were being expanded. During the early modern era (c.1500–1750), incredible discoveries were being made which totally transformed how people thought about the world. Suddenly artists were painting in 3D perspectives, and people learned that our planet, Earth, travels around the Sun. Scientific knowledge soared, religion was reformed and new machines leapt into life, but for the average girl nothing much changed: you were still expected to be a dutiful daughter, obedient wife and devoted mother.

Roles for women in Europe were usually in the home, except for a few jobs which were seen as 'female', such as governesses and midwives. Typical jobs in the home included assisting your husband if he was a farmer, or if you were married to a nobleman you would be expected to entertain visitors to keep your husband's status high. But this was meant to be invisible work, and obviously there would be no pay! Women were expected to be modest in their ways, obey men and give birth to the next generation. In order to challenge these expectations, you would need either your own money or a status which gave you greater freedom and education.

DOS AND DON'TS (BUT MOSTLY DON'TS)

Read the following with caution, you might not like what you hear! The advice below was written in two 'conduct' books published in England in the 17th century, which instructed girls on how to behave. Whether they followed these grim recommendations is another matter!

Don't wear skimpy dresses or 'cobweb attires'.

Avoid gaudy dresses and 'phantasticke fashion' – such as large sleeves.

Don't share any 'strange opinions'.

Don't be proud – remember you will be eaten by worms in the end.

And finally...

Don't have too much fun and laughter or you'll be punished in hell.

SAVVY MERCHANTS

Holland was the only country in the entire world at this time where all girls could go to primary school. Dutch women in the port towns used their maths and literacy education to become bold traders and merchants, running their husbands' businesses while they were away at sea. An English visitor was so amazed that he wrote home to describe how Dutch women chatted to men in the street, visited pubs and even ice-skated through the night! There were also two different types of marriages in Holland. In one, the woman handed over her possessions and rights to her husband, as was usual in the rest of Europe. In the other, she kept her rights as though she were a single woman. Thankfully for us and the rest of Eve's descendents, the second type of marriage eventually became the more popular option!

THE WITCHING HOUR

★✦✦✦✦✦✦✦✦✦✦★✦✦✦✦✦✦★✦✦✦★✦✦✦✦✦✦✦✦★✦✦✦✦★✦✦✦★

The Renaissance era might have begun in Italy, paving the way for new beginnings, but, at the same time, a strange and terrible craze was poised to sweep the western world ... the time of witch hunts and witch trials. A dangerous time for anyone who might be 'too loud' or 'too quarrelsome'. A time when anyone behaving suspiciously could be accused of the crime of being ... a WITCH! Tens of thousands of women – and some men too – were put to death in horrible ways. There was even a witch-hunting manual, *Malleus Maleficarum* or 'The Hammer of Witches', written in Germany. Accusing someone of being a witch could be a way to get rid of a neighbour you didn't like or who you blamed for your own misfortune. If they were too troublesome or unladylike, too 'simple-minded' or independent, or just homeless and 'in the way', it wouldn't be difficult to persuade others that they might be up to no good.

CONFESS!

Not everyone who was accused like this would have been found guilty, but many of those who confessed did so under torture. And sometimes making a confession – even if it wasn't true – could save your life.

In Scotland at the end of the 16th century, a woman named **MARGARET AITKEN** was accused of being a witch, but managed to switch sides by declaring she could tell if someone was a witch...

just by looking at them.

She joined the hunters to save herself from being killed and became known as 'the Great Witch', assisting witch-hunting minister John Cowper by pointing out potential witches. But Margaret's methods were completely random and she was easily tricked when those she had accused one day appeared in front of her the next in different clothes and in a different order; she pointed out a different group as witches. The hunt collapsed, but Cowper and his fellow ministers and magistrates hushed things up. After all, plenty of people Margaret had accused had already been put to death. They might have got away with it if it hadn't been for Marion Walker – a local widow who managed to get hold of the Great Witch's ultimate confession: that she'd made up her accusations to save herself. Marion circulated this information around Glasgow. The magistrates threatened to put anyone who shared it into a 'scold's bridle' – a humiliating metal mask that held down the tongue. But it was too late: brave Marion had made them accountable for their actions.

Salem in Massachusetts in the United States is still famous for being the scene of a horrifying series of witch trials in the 17th century. Two hundred people were accused. Twenty were put to death. Only a few years later, the trials were declared unlawful, and eventually most of the 'witches' were pardoned. But three centuries later, one woman was still left accused: **ELIZABETH JOHNSON JUNIOR**. In 2022, an American middle-school class took up her case. Their teacher helped them collect evidence and present it to the state senator.

Thanks to those children, Elizabeth was finally pardoned 329 years after being accused of witchcraft.

TWO QUEENS

What was it like to be a queen in a man's world? There aren't many people to ask, but two people who knew the job pretty well were Elizabeth I, Queen of England (1533–1603), and Njinga Mbande, Queen of the Mbundu people in southwestern Africa (c.1583–1663), who both led their people during times when women had to fight to be heard.

NJINGA was the sister of the king of the Mbundu people, who lived in what is now Angola in Africa. One day in 1622, her brother sent her to a peace conference with the slave-trading Portuguese. The Portuguese governor had a comfy chair to sit on, but Njinga was expected to sit on the floor. She knew this was so that she would look less powerful than him. No chance! Njinga wasn't having that, and ordered one of her subjects to get down on their hands and knees to make a chair for her. Now she was the governor's equal. Njinga's actions were so impressive that when her brother died, Njinga was elected to become ruler. It didn't come easily, though – not everyone agreed and some men who opposed the vote even joined the Portuguese army against her.

Although Njinga became a Christian like the Portuguese, she didn't want to make any further concessions that would allow them to control her country. A war began between them that lasted 30 years. Even into her sixties, Njinga was still leading her troops into battle. Eventually she successfully signed a peace treaty with the Portuguese. Despite all her enemies, she died peacefully in her eighties.

Njinga's father had encouraged her to train with the army and to sit in with him on court sessions to learn as much as she could about running the country before she became queen. Perhaps he suspected she might one day be called on to rule instead of other male members of the family...

In England, King Henry VIII was desperate to have a son who would inherit the throne. So when his second wife, Anne Boleyn, became pregnant, the king was excited. But then came ... a GIRL! What use was that?! Little did he know that little **ELIZABETH** would end up ruling England for almost 45 years. Like Njinga, Elizabeth also had many enemies. Unlike Njinga she didn't go into battle herself, but she did deliver a famous speech inspiring her navy to defeat the attempted Spanish invasion in 1588. There were also plenty of people close to Elizabeth who wanted her dead. Some wanted to get rid of her so her Catholic cousin could rule instead, while the Earl of Essex, who had been in a romantic relationship with her, wanted power for himself. Well, Elizabeth didn't put up with any of this backstabbing. Both cousin and earl ended up executed when the plots were discovered.

Elizabeth had many other suitors too, but she never found 'the one'. The arts were her true love, and she even had Shakespeare perform private plays for her at court. There are many portraits of her with a huge ruff to make her look powerful and a painted white face to hide her smallpox scars. Just like celebrity photoshoots today, the portraits we have left are the ones she liked – any that made her look ugly, she destroyed!

When Elizabeth made a speech to her navy before they went into battle against the invading Spanish fleet, she said, 'I know I have the body of a weak and feeble woman; but I have the heart and stomach of a king.' Whilst this might not sound ultra feminist in today's world,

Elizabeth was out to prove that she could defend her country just as well as a man could.

THE JOSEON KINGDOM

Imagine having to stay inside your home because you were the property of your father or husband, or even your brother! This was the unfortunate life for women in the Joseon dynasty. Joseon was an independent kingdom in Korea founded at the end of the 14th century. Due to the strict gender roles of the Confucian religion, women were expected to be modest, beautiful and subservient. If you had to leave the house, you would have to cover your body and face and turn your head away if you saw anyone. There was even a rule that boys and girls couldn't sit together after the age of seven, and the government issued special booklets with instructions on how to behave.

As a very young girl in Joseon, you might be chosen to be a servant in the royal palace. Your working life would start at the ripe old age of five and you would be trained to work in one of many strictly defined departments, doing tasks such as lighting candles or sewing. There was even a department for rewarding and punishing your fellow servants. If you were lucky you MIGHT get paid, but if you were an enslaved girl you would be given the lowliest jobs. The only chance to make a career of sorts was if you were able to become a healer. Due to religious reasons women couldn't be seen by male doctors, so women healers were needed at the palace to treat female members of the court. This was a rare chance to get an education and read medical texts, and you might even be rewarded by an increase in status if your treatments were successful.

If you were born into the *yangban* (the noble class), you were important inside your own house, but still weren't allowed to go outside during the day.

Instead you had to wait until the men were inside at night and then go out covered up.

You were brought up to be modest and not stand out, and you were encouraged not to get too attached to your family as you would be leaving them to move in with your husband's household as soon as you were married. After that your main duty would be to have a son. If you didn't, your husband could divorce you, or he could try to have a son with someone else instead.

The greatest achievement for a women in the Joseon kingdom was to be given the Virtuous Woman Award. This was usually presented to those who stayed single after their husband died. Sometimes, in extreme cases, women killed themselves to show their loyalty. Then the award would be given to the dead woman's family.

The most famous woman from the Joseon kingdom was **SHIN SAIMDANG**, who was born in 1504. A painter, embroiderer, poet and calligrapher, her beautiful flower and insect paintings can be seen in museums around the world today. How did Saimdang achieve all this in such a strict society? We don't know a lot about Saimdang, but it is said she was encouraged to paint by her family. This determined and super-talented woman will not be forgotten as she is celebrated all over Korea as the face of the 50,000 won note.

REVOLUTIONARY REBELS

In 1789, France was turned upside down as poverty and discontent spiralled into a revolution that would go down in history as one of the greatest. Many women rioted over food prices as they struggled to feed their families. Women even triggered a famous march on Versailles, a royal palace about 18 kilometres west of the capital city, as a protest against the king and queen. It started in Paris, where women in a market were complaining about the price of bread. It seemed especially unfair when a slap-up banquet had just taken place at the Palace of Versailles. One woman started beating a drum – literally drumming up support – and before long a riot had started. The crowds grew and 7,000 people ended up marching to Versailles to confront the king and queen. The royal family were forced to return to Paris, where they eventually met their deaths. The revolution was underway and a new regime began.

For a while anything seemed possible, and women felt they had a better chance of gaining more rights. Some women formed a group called the *Cercle Social* (Social Circle) and campaigned for better divorce, property and inheritance laws.

OLYMPE DE GOUGES was a bold playwright who wanted to see change for women, and she wrote a book called *Declaration of the Rights of Women and of the Female Citizen*. The new government, however, really didn't like anyone protesting against them. Olympe was thrown into prison and her head was cut off by guillotine, all for the small crime of writing her book.

The most famous woman of the revolution was **CHARLOTTE CORDAY**, who assassinated the politician Jean-Paul Marat by stabbing him while he was having a bath. Women formed political clubs such as the Society of Revolutionary Republican Women (*Le Club* for short), but the government must have been worried about their activities because all women's clubs were banned in 1793. Women could even go to prison for complaining about the price of food, bad-mouthing officials or wearing trousers.

The revolutionary governments did eventually give women equal rights in divorce and inheriting property, but they did not give them the political rights they wanted. Despite the revolution promising freedom and equality for all, French women were only finally given the vote in 1944.

One protest outside a temple in 1794 involved a group of peasant women who all turned their backs at the same time and bared their bottoms!

The reason? A new religion invented by harsh revolutionary leader Robespierre which he called the Cult of the Supreme Being. Others must have shared the same feelings as the bottom-barers, as the new religion never took off and died soon after, just like Robespierre himself, in fact.

FACTORY GIRLS

The world reached an important milestone in the 1800s when the population grew to more than one billion! The 19th century was marked by endings and beginnings: violent wars and revolutions ended monarchies and overturned governments, while innovative new technology began to emerge. A global flu pandemic killed one million people, but the world became more connected as travel became faster and more efficient. The Industrial Revolution brought new machinery and ways of working, which led to huge changes in how people lived. Rather than working in the home or on the farm, large numbers of women trooped off to jobs in mills, factories and even mines, working long hours for lower pay than the men (obviously!).

THE LOWELL OFFERING was a newspaper written by the 'mill girls' who lived and worked at the cotton mills built by Francis Lowell in Massachusetts, USA. The teenagers wrote prose and poems about their lives and how they enjoyed being part of a community, but the reality was a little different. They had been promised an exciting life in the city with new opportunities and independence, but actually had to work for 12 hours a day, six days a week. Their lives were ruled by the factory bell. There was a campaign to reduce the length of the working day, and finally the mill owners agreed – the girls would only have to work for ... 11 hours instead! Amazingly they still found time to write for the newspaper, and their writing surprised many readers who were sceptical about the abilities of 'factory girls'. They even received a compliment from one of the most famous writers of all time: Charles Dickens!

The Bryant and May factory in East London employed many young girls to make matches. Conditions were hard with long hours and small salaries, and girls could even be fined for being untidy at work. If you worked from home, you would even have to buy your own materials. The worst part was that white phosphorus was used,

a dangerous chemical that could cause 'phossy jaw'. Making matches meant you could lose your teeth, your jaw bone and sometimes your life. And there was no escape: you even had to take your lunch break in the same room where the chemical was used.

In 1888 a socialist reform group called the Fabian Society decided to spread the word about the bad conditions and interviewed some of the girls. Campaigner **ANNIE BESANT** then published an article about them. The factory denied everything and tried to get the girls to sign statements saying the story had been made up. The brave girls refused and, with support from some MPs and the newspapers,

around 1,400 match girls went on strike, refusing to work until conditions were improved.

The mass walkout and bad publicity worked. The company's directors agreed to all demands, and the announcement was greeted with cheers and applause. A union was formed and the success inspired other unions, leading eventually to the forming of the Labour Party in Britain. Bryant and May were fined for neglecting their workers, and in 1908 a bill was passed, banning white phosphorus matches for good.

The seemingly powerless matchgirls had found strength together and brought about huge change.

THE ARMY OF THE AGOJIE

Meanwhile, in West Africa, in the kingdom of Dahomey (present-day Benin), a terrifying army raided its enemies by night. They burned villages and sold their victims as slaves, or beheaded the captives and took the heads back to the king. This violent and powerful army was made up of up to 6,000 warriors called the Agojie.

And the Agojie were all women.

This fierce female army probably started as elephant hunters, but when too many male soldiers were killed in ongoing wars against neighbouring kingdoms and European settlers, the women stepped up to become warriors. Not all the women did this of their own free will. Some were enslaved, or were rebels rejected by their families, or were too poor to have any other options. After becoming an Agojie, however, they were treated like royalty.

The Dahomey people referred to the Agojie as 'our mothers' and they lived in a special section of the palace with their own servants. They were also automatically *ahosi* (wives of the king), even though they weren't allowed to have any relationships. This meant they were part of the king's grand council. Although the king still had absolute power, his *ahosi* could advise him.

The palace was almost entirely female at night, with no men allowed inside after sunset apart from the king himself.

Training for this formidable female army was tough. It included killing prisoners and scrambling over huge walls of thorns. If you made it, you were rewarded with a thorn belt – and plenty of scratches! Exercises like this toughened up the warriors and made them brave. But their greatest skill was the ability to sneak up on the enemy completely unseen.

By the end of the 19th century, after repeatedly battling against invading French armies, the Agojie were no more. The kingdom was controlled by France, which had different ideas of how a woman should behave. The Dahomey people lost their way of life, and some ended up as living tourist attractions, performing their ceremonies for visitors to gape at.

DO NOT TOUCH!

When an Agojie left the palace, a slave would ring a bell to let people know she was coming. This was so they could keep back and look away to show respect. Keeping your distance was very important – if you touched an Agojie, it could mean death!

THE LAST AGOJIE

The last surviving Agojie was called **NAWI**. She died in 1979 and was over 100 years old. She told a visiting historian that she remembered fighting against the French as a teenager in 1892.

SCIENCE AGAINST THE ODDS

Around the world, women who wanted a career in science were still battling to get into higher education. They weren't allowed to go to university which made a career in science almost impossible. But women scientists were determined – so much so that they sometimes had to set up their own institutions so they could attend them.

One institution was set up by **SOPHIA JEX-BLAKE**, a Scottish maths teacher who was trying to go to university. She thought there must be more like her, so she placed an advert in the local newspaper. Six women answered and together they applied to the Edinburgh University court. The 'Edinburgh Seven', as they became known, were successful and, in 1869, they became the first women to be accepted to study at a British university. But it wasn't the easiest of journeys into education. Their fellow students definitely did not make them feel welcome. The male students threw mud at them and even smuggled a live sheep into the exam hall to cause chaos and ruin their chances. Sophia took the ringleader to court and won, but was left with an enormous legal bill. Then, after all that, the university decided at the end of their courses that it wouldn't award them degrees. It was back to court again for Sophia, but this time the ruling went against her: the women could study, but not qualify. So that's what they did. Sophia finished her course and went to London for more training, where she avoided further battles by starting her own school! The London School of Medicine for Women opened in 1874, and Sophia was its student. Two years later, MPs voted to let women qualify in medicine after all. Finally, in 2019, Edinburgh University awarded the Edinburgh Seven their medical degrees – 150 years after they finished there!

ALL WORK AND NO PAY

Being a governess or tutor was one of the few acceptable jobs for 'respectable' women. But Sophia Jex-Blake's father was so horrified at the idea of his daughter working for a living that he would only let her teach maths if she did it for free!

THE DINOSAUR DIGGER

Many families in the 19th century lived in such poor and cramped conditions that it was common for children to die of diseases like smallpox and measles. So the odds were already against **MARY ANNING**, who was born in 1799 in Lyme Regis in Dorset, England. She was one of the few children in her family who survived, despite even being struck by lightning as a toddler! She spent a lot of time with her father, and they roamed the beach together collecting fossils to sell to tourists. Other than learning to read, Mary did not have much schooling – but she did know a lot about fossils. Her father died when she was just 11, so Mary carried on fossil hunting in order to support her family. One day her brother found a strange-looking skull. Mary spent months painstakingly digging out the rest of the outline. They had found a monster! This huge beast turned out to be an *Ichthyosaurus*, a reptile who lived in the ocean.

Mary went on to discover a complete *Plesiosaurus* and even a pterodactyl! The male scientists who bought her finds took all the credit themselves, but today Mary is recognized as an extraordinary palaeontologist and also as a pioneer of the study of fossilized poo!

Mary's dinosaurs are now proudly on display at the Lyme Regis Museum, the Natural History Museum in London and the Museum of Natural History in Oxford, with proper accreditation, of course.

VICTORIA AND THE VICTORIANS

Early on a June morning in 1837 in England, a teenage girl was woken by her mother and told she had visitors. **VICTORIA** hurriedly put on her dressing-gown and went into her sitting room, where two of the most important people in the country were waiting with grave faces. The Lord Chamberlain and the Archbishop of Canterbury gave her the life-changing news: Victoria's uncle was dead, which meant she was now...

Queen of the United Kingdom and the British Empire.

As a princess in line to the throne, Victoria had grown up in luxury in Kensington Palace but was treated like a china doll. She wasn't even allowed to walk down a flight of stairs without someone holding her hand in case she fell. Zero independence! A small woman, Victoria had to fight against being underestimated. She also had to learn who to trust and where to get the best advice. Like all royals her marriage was arranged for her, but luckily for Victoria she was totally in love with her beloved Prince Albert, and they went on to have nine children and 42 grandchildren! Albert died unexpectedly in 1861 leaving Victoria to mourn him for the remaining 40 years of her life. She wore black every day and it was ten years before she started appearing in public again.

The British Empire expanded hugely during Victoria's reign. Eventually Victoria ruled India and large parts of Africa and the Caribbean as well as Australia, New Zealand and Canada. The British believed their presence would improve the places they controlled, but removing existing rulers and imposing British rule came at a great cost for the countries involved.

One of the Indian princes the British dethroned moved to England and had a daughter called **PRINCESS SOPHIA DULEEP SINGH**. Queen Victoria took an interest in the baby and became her godmother. But she was not amused at what Sophia did next! Victoria believed it would be a huge mistake to give women the vote (despite being the most powerful woman in the country at the time), but Princess Sophia campaigned for votes for women and was a key player in women's suffrage.

A VICTORIAN HOUSEMAID'S DAY

At the other end of the social scale from royalty were the working class. If you were a servant, your days were long with little time off. The job was so gruelling that when factory work became available there was a shortage of servants as it was seen as an easier option!

6am – Clean out fireplaces and light fires. Shake rugs and rub down furniture.

8am – Change dirty apron and take hot water to bedrooms. Eat quick breakfast.

9am – Open bedroom windows, air or change beds, empty washstands and chamber pots, replace towels, tidy rooms. Sweep passages and dust furniture.

11am – Quick drink for lunch. Turn out rooms to clean, depending on rota.

1pm – Check all fires and generally tidy. Sewing and mending – a chance to sit down.

5pm – Teatime with staff in kitchen.

7pm – Tidy ground floor while family have dinner. Get beds ready, check fires.

9pm – Suppertime.

10pm – Take up hot-water bottles to bedrooms. Go to own cold bed ready for another day.

WOMEN AND SLAVERY

If you were an enslaved person in the 18th and early 19th centuries, your life would be full of abuse and punishment. Many were captured through wars or slave raids in Africa and then sold abroad, forced to work as servants and labourers with no pay and no freedom. Children were taken from their parents and anyone born into slavery was automatically a slave, too. In theory you could buy your freedom, but with what money? Enslaved women were also expected to 'breed' to increase the slave workforce, and were often forced to do so by their enslavers.

During the 19th century, slavery was gradually abolished round the world thanks to campaigners, many of whom were women who had escaped from slavery themselves. By sharing their stories and exposing the awful horrors they had endured, brave women helped persuade politicians that slavery should be brought to an end. Some of those women were:

MARY PRINCE, the first Black woman to have her writing published in Britain about her life as an enslaved person in Bermuda and Antigua in the Caribbean.

. . . .

ELLEN CRAFT, who disguised herself as a white man while her husband William pretended to be her slave, to escape from captivity in Georgia, USA.

. . . .

IDA B WELLS-BARNETT, who was born into slavery in Mississippi, USA, and became a teacher, journalist and anti-lynching campaigner.

. . . .

HARRIET TUBMAN, who was only 12 when she tried to stop her enslaver beating someone and was hit by a weight as punishment. She escaped through the 'Underground Railroad', a network of safe routes and safehouses, and returned to free many others. During the Civil War she was a nurse and spy, becoming the first African-American to help lead an armed raid which freed enslaved people. She also campaigned for votes for women and founded a home for the elderly.

. . . .

SOJOURNER TRUTH, who was bought and sold four times as a slave in New York. She escaped and became a preacher, renaming herself Sojourner Truth to represent her new life. She travelled the country giving rousing anti-slavery speeches and supporting women's rights. She also helped freed enslaved people find jobs and rebuild their lives.

SOJOURNER'S SPEECH

Sojourner Truth was known for her powerful speeches. In 1851 she made a speech to the Akron Women's Conference. Sojourner talked about her strength and all the trials she had endured. She then reminded the audience that she was a woman. Couldn't she do just as much as a man? To those who argued that men were superior to women because Jesus was a man, Sojourner argued that Jesus owed his existence to a woman – his mother Mary.

The speech became famously known as the 'Ain't I a Woman?' speech.

SUBVERSIVE SISTERS

There was a surge of books published by female writers in the 19th century, as women's voices began to be acknowledged and heard. Even so, some authors felt they had to publish under a man's name to be taken seriously...

George Eliot, who wrote *Middlemarch*, was really **MARY ANN EVANS**.

Another George, this time the French novelist George Sand, was really **AMANTINE LUCILE AURORE DUPIN**. Her work was more renowned than Victor Hugo at the time.

A. M. Barnard was **LOUISA MAY ALCOTT**, who wrote *Little Women*.

The mysterious brothers Currer, Ellis and Acton Bell were really the shy **BRONTË** sisters **CHARLOTTE**, **EMILY** and **ANNE**. Not even their publishers knew until Charlotte and Anne turned up in person and took them by surprise!

Poetry was considered just about acceptable for women to write but 'literature cannot be the business of a woman's life'. These were the scathing words written to Charlotte Brontë by the poet Robert Southey. Thankfully she refused to believe him, and Charlotte and her two sisters went on to write classics such as *Jane Eyre* and the powerfully original *Wuthering Heights*.

REVIEWS FOR WUTHERING HEIGHTS

Emily Brontë shocked reviewers with her book, even when they thought she was a man. Imagine what they would have said if they'd known she was a woman all along!

'...the incidents are too coarse and disagreeable...'

'...shocking pictures of the worst forms of humanity...'

'...the only consolation which we have in reflecting upon it is that it will never be generally read.'

'This is a strange book.'

READING IS BAD FOR YOU!

Imagine being told that reading is bad for you. That was the case for girls and women at the time who were advised to stick to religious or improving books only. Girls born into noble families were luckier – they had family libraries to dip into and a hunger for reading and learning developed. Doctors were alarmed and warned of hysteria as a result – reading could be dangerous! Novels were supposed to set good examples for how young women should behave, which is why stories such as *Wuthering Heights*, with its wild characters and extreme emotions, were so scandalous. Even visiting a public library was not 'the done thing' for a woman on her own. Despite all these barriers, women's literacy levels were steadily improving. The power of reading was opening the door to knowledge and the next step in the *Shevolution* story: the vote.

THE STORY OF VOTES FOR WOMEN

While women started writing, reading and learning more, their rights were still pretty much non-existent. Society's views about women at the time meant there was a lot to fight for!

WOMEN: *"We want the right to further education."*

WOMEN: *"We want the right to equal pay and jobs."*

WOMEN: *"We want the right to own property after marriage."*

WOMEN: *"We want the right to keep our children after divorce."*

WOMEN: *"We want the right to have a legal identity."*

WOMEN: *"We want the right to vote so we can achieve all the above."*

SOCIETY: *"Women's minds are too fragile."*

SOCIETY: *"Working-class women can do manual work. Middle- and upper-class women are too refined and should confine themselves to gentle tasks or supervising others."*

SOCIETY: *"Women don't need property. Besides, their husbands can look after it much better than they can!"*

SOCIETY: *"A man should take his own children from a failed marriage – after all, it's the woman's fault that it didn't work out!"*

SOCIETY: *"A woman is not a separate person once she's married, so why should she have her own rights?"*

SOCIETY: *"Women don't need the vote – their fathers and husbands know what's best for them. Anyway, they are far too busy managing the home to be interested in politics."*

Women realized they could be more powerful if they came together, and the first women's rights convention was held in Seneca Falls, USA, in 1848. It was organized by **ELIZABETH CADY STANTON** and three of her friends, after deciding they'd had enough of the unfair treatment of women. There was outrage at the idea of a women's convention, but this acted as brilliant publicity. Other conventions soon followed and societies began to form such as the National Society for Women's Suffrage in Britain. Lobbying of parliament began and more and more women and some men joined the cause. In Britain, campaigning became more violent, with women putting their lives in danger to draw attention to their fight.

The first country to give women equal rights to vote was New Zealand in 1893, thanks to women like **KATE SHEPPARD**. Kate organized a 'monster petition', so long that it was rolled around a broom handle and then dramatically unrolled down the centre of the debating chamber in parliament. Australia was the next country to give women the vote, with Finland, Norway and Denmark soon after. The rest of the world followed over the next century. But some countries resisted for a long time. Indigenous women in Australia and Canada were not allowed to vote until the 1960s, and Black South Africans could not vote until 1994.

Most recently in 2015, Saudi Arabia finally gave women the right to vote in local elections (currently the only type of elections the country holds).

Being permitted to vote doesn't always mean you can. In some countries where women have fewer rights, they are discouraged from voting by being intimidated or threatened. And in the countries of Brunei and Eritrea nobody can vote at all, man or woman.

'...women are not capable of holding their own in the rough contests of the world.'

Editor of *The Times*, an English newspaper, in 1868

WOMEN BELONG IN THE KITCHEN!

WOMEN ARE FRAGILE!

WOMEN RISE UP

WOMEN'S RIGHTS

VOTES FOR WOMEN

FIGHTING FOR THE VOTE

★ ✦ ★ ✦ ★ ✦ ★ ✦ ★ ✦ ★ ✦ ★ ✦ ★ ✦ ★ ✦ ★ ✦ ★ ✦ ★ ✦ ★ ✦ ★ ✦ ★ ✦ ★ ✦ ★ ✦ ★ ✦ ★ ✦ ★

Turbulent times were ahead in the 20th century. Millions would be killed in two world wars, and communism and democracy would fight it out in the 'Cold War'. Meanwhile, humanity would eat up the planet's resources at an ever-increasing rate.

At the beginning of the 20th century, women had achieved voting rights in a few countries, but there was still a long way to go in places like the UK and the USA. Peaceful campaigning had not worked and some women felt it was time to take more extreme action. These activists were known as suffragettes. Some of their protests included:

- *Chaining themselves to railings*
- *Window-smashing*
- *Bombing and arson attacks*
- *Chemical attacks*
- *Hunger strikes in prison*

Women were not only campaigning for the vote, they were declaring war on society and they were changing the public's view of how a woman behaved. Some peaceful campaigners disagreed with their methods. Did the suffragettes help their cause or turn the public against them? We don't know for sure, as something then happened that turned everything on its head: the First World War. Imprisoned suffragettes were released to help with the war effort, and the contribution of women overall showed they meant business. For many countries, this was the time when voting for women was finally granted.

THE TRAGEDY AT EPSOM

At Epsom Racecourse in England, there was a dramatic scene: the suffragette **EMILY DAVISON** hurled herself in front of the king's horse in the middle of a race.

Emily died from her injuries and the jockey on the horse was horrified. At the time, people believed that Emily ended her life to gain publicity for women's right to vote, but recently historians have been able to look more closely at footage of the event. They saw that rather than trying to bring the horse down or kill herself, Emily was hoping to attach a suffragette flag to the horse. She also had a return railway ticket in her pocket.

In the early 20th century, women in most states in America still didn't have the vote. The National Woman's Party decided to demonstrate outside the White House every day until they got the attention of the president, Woodrow Wilson. After ten months of this they began to be attacked by mobs and arrested for blocking the road, but they didn't give up. One member, **ALICE PAUL**, was arrested seven times. In one night in November 1917, 33 women were arrested at once. They were imprisoned in terrible conditions and treated brutally by the guards. When they were finally released, the president decided the vote should be given to women in all states, not just some.

SELMA LAGERLÖF from Sweden became the first woman to win the Nobel Prize for Literature in 1909. But incredibly, her country did not allow her, or any other women, to vote. In 1917, peaceful protestors used this to make a powerful point. They held up three photographs of people who couldn't vote: a male prisoner, a male psychiatric patient and Selma. Swedish women got the vote in 1921.

'It is not only war we have declared, we are fighting for a revolution.'

Christabel Pankhurst

DARING TO DISCOVER

Despite the turbulence, wars and protests, huge strides were beginning to be made for women in politics, the arts and education. Determined to be heard, women were smashing the myth that females were delicate and feeble and were making some amazing – and sometimes explosive – discoveries.

In 1902, **HERTHA AYRTON**, a Jewish woman from London, published *The Electric Arc*, an important text on electric lighting. She went on to make vital discoveries in electricity and registered no fewer than 26 inventions! One of them was a special fan to repel deadly mustard gas from the trenches in the First World War.

American **NETTIE STEVENS** graduated from a university in Pennsylvania in 1903 with a PhD in cytology (a branch of biology that focuses on cells). She later discovered that sex is determined by X and Y chromosomes. Shockingly, the credit went to a male scientist who was studying at the same time.

MARIE CURIE of Poland and then France became the first woman to win the Nobel Prize for Physics in 1903. She won another for chemistry eight years later. Marie studied radioactivity and x-rays, and developed a mobile x-ray machine she nicknamed the mini-Curie. It was used to help treat soldiers in the First World War, saving many lives.

In 1913, **CHIKA KURODA** was the first woman to walk through the doors of the chemistry department as a student at Tohoku Imperial University in Sendai, Japan. She became a professor specializing in natural pigments, and discovered crystals in onion skin, which were then used to develop a blood-pressure drug.

English-American **CECILIA PAYNE-GAPOSCHKIN** looked through a telescope in 1925 and discovered what stars are made of (hydrogen and helium) by observing their light waves.

By 1926, Austrian scientist **LISE MEITNER** secured a research job at the University of Berlin. She was unpaid and given a small room in the basement. Twelve years later she jointly discovered nuclear fission, leading to the development of the atomic bomb.

The rise of the 'office job' meant that women started to be employed as typists and bookkeepers, keeping track of money and accounts. This was a way into the working world for women, especially for those gifted at maths. The very best were used by scientific institutions and governments as human 'computers'! Women were showing they could make important calculations and contribute to exciting research, such as cataloguing stars at the Harvard Observatory.

THE WAR TO END ALL WARS

The First World War was a huge conflict that involved nations in Europe, Africa, Asia, Australasia and North and South America. The turmoil raged for four terrible years. New technologies such as machine guns, chemical weapons, tank warfare and fighter planes caused devastation, killing over 16 million people. It was known as the Great War, 'the war to end all wars', although sadly that didn't turn out to be the case.

All men who were fit to fight were conscripted into the armed forces, meaning women were needed to fill the jobs they left behind. Women worked in munitions factories, patrolled the streets as police officers, worked as drivers and engineers on the buses and railways, and took up many other traditionally male jobs. The need for practical work clothes meant the end of long skirts and tightly pulled-in waists.

Trousers (and pockets!) were on their way!

One of the most vital jobs during the war was making weapons and ammunition. Munitions factories employed thousands of women, and nurseries were set up to look after their children. It was dangerous work, which brought with it serious risks of illness and even sudden explosions. Workers were encouraged to keep fit and healthy, and in Britain women's football became popular, with matches attracting large crowds. Sadly this did not last long. The Football Association banned the women's game in 1921 and did not lift the ban for another 50 years.

Many women were keen to fight for their country. In Britain the women's army, air force and navy were formed and over 100,000 women joined up. In other countries, some women disguised themselves as men in order to join the forces. Russian teenager **ZOYA SMIRNOW** was only 16 when she and her friends dressed up as boys to enlist in the Russian army, while **VIKTORIA SAVS** also dressed as a boy and served with the Austrian army, winning several medals for bravery. The girls were only found out when they were injured and had to be examined in hospital. **STEPHANIE HOLLENSTEIN** enrolled into the Austrian army using the name Stephan. After a few months she was found out, but managed to get accepted as a female war artist instead, recording scenes from the battlefield. Later she became a professional painter.

The countries involved in the First World War faced the tragic loss of around one in ten men. Women lost husbands, fiancés, brothers and sons. Soldiers returning from the war needed jobs to go back to, and most women were forced to give up their new roles. The world tried to rebuild itself, not knowing that only 21 years later another world war would darken the skies.

'My good lady, go home and sit still.'

This was the reply by the British War Office when Scottish doctor **ELSIE INGLIS** wrote to them offering to help her country. Elsie did not take no for an answer.

Instead of sitting still, she took herself to Serbia to treat the wounded and founded the Scottish Women's Hospitals.

DANGEROUS NURSING

It wasn't just those on the front line in the First World War who put their lives at risk. Nursing was a dangerous and harrowing occupation. Working in a field hospital you would spend 12 hours a day dressing wounds, fighting infection and, in the most hopeless cases, making the dying as comfortable as they could be. Sometimes after major battles you would be working 24 hours a day as the hospital became a living hell. Through all the trauma you had to stay positive and professional. Hobby clubs and concerts were organized to keep your spirits up. You also got one half-day off a week, if you were lucky.

Some nurses went beyond their medical roles. In Belgium, **EDITH CAVELL** not only treated soldiers from both sides, she also helped many Allied soldiers to escape from enemy territory and rejoin their troops. Sadly she was betrayed by a spy and Edith was executed by German firing squad.

Good friends **ELSIE KNOCKER** and **MAIRI CHISHOLM** were keen English motorcyclists. When war broke out they signed up together to work as ambulance drivers in Belgium and France, taking wounded soldiers from the battlefield to the hospitals. A speedy journey was vital in order to save lives – literally every second counted. The journey had to be shortened somehow, and Elsie and Mairi decided that treatment needed to be closer to the scene. They raised funds and set up their own treatment centre right by the front line, working in the cellar of a house for safety, and even living there. For three years they treated men from both sides, carrying them off the battlefield on their backs, before gas attacks forced them to leave. They both joined the air force for the rest of the war, and Elsie was a Squadron Officer in the Second World War as well.

New technologies meant new weapons, and new weapons meant new types of injuries and new treatments.

FLORENCE NIGHTINGALE, **MARY SEACOLE** and **CLARA BARTON** had made great improvements in nursing care in the previous century. Now female nurses were at the forefront of new advances, using oxygen to treat gassed lungs, bathing gas-blinded eyes and giving the new tetanus injections as well as maintaining complex equipment for keeping wounds moist. They also needed to keep patients stable for transportation to other hospitals or safer areas, travelling with them in ambulances, trains and even barge hospitals.

MEDDLESOME MILLIE

Some aristocratic women who had money and wanted to act quickly set up their own hospitals in France and Belgium. One of these was the Duchess of Sutherland from England. Her nickname was Meddlesome Millie, which shows how society labelled strong, decisive women at the time.

'The horrors of war are appalling.'

Nurse Beatrice Tanner's wartime diary, 1914

AN UNCERTAIN TIME

✦✦✦✦✦✦✦✦✦✦✦✦✦✦✦✦✦✦✦✦✦✦✦✦✦✦✦✦✦✦✦✦✦✦✦✦

In the years following the First World War, the world struggled to rebuild itself, and civil wars (where a country is at war with itself) continued. Russia's civil war resulted in it absorbing other countries to become the Soviet Union, a communist state, while in Germany Adolf Hitler began his rise to becoming the leader of the Nazi party.

Despite all the uncertainty, this next decade was nicknamed the 'Roaring Twenties' because it was the era of dazzling silent movie starlets, sleek motor cars, trendy clubs and high fashion. For working-class women this glamorous life was all a dream, to be seen at a distance, if at all.

If you were a young stylish woman from a well-off family, you might be called a 'flapper'. Rebelling against the dour Edwardian fashions of your mother's generation, you would have short, bobbed hair, shorter skirts (trousers were very daring) and an exciting nightlife dancing the Charleston and drinking cocktails in the new jazz clubs. Women enjoyed smoking, which was seen as good for the throat (which is definitely not true!) and used elegant cigarette holders. The flapper girl was a popular image in the media, but in reality not many women had the opportunity to follow this lifestyle.

Fashions were drastically changing. The restricting corset, a tightly laced undergarment, which had held in so many women's waists and restricted their movements and breathing, was on its way out at last. This was partly due to new trends but also because of lack of clothing materials after the war.

During the 1920s, the familiar devices we see in our homes today began to appear. Vacuum cleaners, electric irons, fridges and washing machines were all marketed as miraculous labour-saving devices. But rather than freeing 'housewives' to work outside the home, the pressure was on to be an even more perfect homemaker with the perfect tools. Jobs were for poor women who did not have any other choice and careers, for the most part, were for men.

There was one surprising place in the 1920s where women dominated: Hollywood.

Woman such as **DOROTHY PARKER**, **FRANCES MARION** and **LOIS WEBER** were both directors and screenwriters, and were among the highest paid silent filmmakers of the day. A woman – **DOROTHY ARZNER** – even invented the boom microphone, a way to record sound during filming by suspending a specially shaped microphone above people's heads.

Some actresses had great power. **MARY PICKFORD** was not only a star on screen but produced films and co-founded United Artists, a film production company complete with pink toilets. She also raised money for actors in need. Meanwhile, in independent cinema, women like **ELOYCE GIST**, a Black producer, and **MARION WONG**, a Chinese-American artist, were making their own films outside the Hollywood system. When the technology for films with sound arrived and silent films became 'talkies', women were edged out as the film industry exploded into a huge money-making machine.

BREAKING AWAY

The next decade began with the Great Depression. Discontent and unrest pushed countries into conflict and by the end of the difficult 1930s, the world was at war again.

The Great Depression was a sudden plunge in the world's economies. Banks and businesses closed and people lost their jobs. But while many men were unemployed, women's employment actually increased. Jobs traditionally seen as 'women's work' such as nursing, teaching, clerical work and domestic service were less affected by the Depression. In some cases this meant women took over as the main earners for their families, plus there were more single women after the war who needed to support themselves. However, if women were married and their husbands already had a job, they were labelled 'selfish' for taking the job away from a man. And if they did work, they were paid less than a man and had fewer benefits.

THE FIRST LADY

ELEANOR ROOSEVELT was the American president's wife (the 'First Lady') at the time of the Depression. She persuaded her husband to hire more female staff and made a rousing speech to encourage American women through the hard times.

FEARLESS FEMALE ADVENTURERS

Despite the Depression, women were still battling to achieve new ambitions and reach new heights – literally.

AMELIA EARHART was a daring American pilot who became passionate about planes while watching them flying as she was nursing in the First World War. When Amelia got her pilot's licence only 15 other women in the world had them, including **BESSIE COLEMAN**, the inspirational first African-American female pilot who died in a crash in 1926. During the 1930s, Amelia set lots of records such

as being the first woman to fly solo across the Atlantic Ocean. Like Bessie she also died doing what she loved: she disappeared in 1937 during a flight around the world. Amelia's death remains a mystery.

Englishwoman **AMY JOHNSON** was another record breaker. Inspired to fly after visiting an aerodrome, in 1930 she became the first woman to fly solo from England to Australia in a small plane she called *Jason*. Her route was planned by drawing a straight line with a ruler on a map! Amy was killed in the Second World War, but was a huge celebrity in her time. People even asked for the 'Amy Johnson haircut' so that they could look like her.

On the ground but still breaking boundaries, intrepid African-American author **ZORA NEALE HURSTON** travelled solo to Haiti and Jamaica in the 1930s to study Black folklore and anthropology. She researched voodoo culture and took part in a ceremony where she mixed her blood with rattlesnake blood! Zora wrote articles, plays and novels, and her work was centred around Black lives and experiences. As a woman of colour (both her parents had been enslaved), she was not paid well and died in poverty. Today her work is read in American schools and around the world.

SPIES AND SACRIFICES

The Second World War dominated the first half of the 1940s. Millions died in the conflict, including six million Jewish people who were exterminated in concentration camps and gas chambers by the Nazis in what became known as the Holocaust. After the war ended, countries still struggled to find peace. Germany and Korea were divided in two by the Allied forces, and China, after civil war, became a communist dictatorship.

As well as taking on the jobs left by soldiers during the war, women could now serve in the armed forces. They weren't put on the front lines, but did vital 'backroom' jobs such as administration or working as cooks, drivers and nurses. Many women also worked in intelligence, computing and codebreaking, while British woman **BEATRICE SHILLING** was an outstanding aircraft engineer. British Prime Minister Winston Churchill's daughter **MARY** joined the ATS (Auxiliary Territorial Service). Even **PRINCESS ELIZABETH**, the future queen of the United Kingdom, became a driver and mechanic during the war while still in her teens.

Female resistance fighters and spies were also recruited. Many of these brave and selfless women lost their lives, including:

VERA LEIGH, adopted as a baby in England, who became a dress designer in France before working undercover as a spy and courier. Posing as a milliner (a hat maker), she used hat boxes to transport documents. Vera was captured by the Nazis and put to death in one of their concentration camps.

....

NOOR INAYAT KHAN, who was descended from an Indian sultan, grew up in Paris and wrote children's stories. Escaping from occupied France, she returned there to operate a resistance radio network and report back to Britain. Though captured and tortured, she refused to give information to the Nazis and was shot.

....

VIOLETTE SZABO, half French and half English, whose language skills, athleticism and fearlessness made her a perfect spy. Parachuting into occupied France, she reported back to Britain where her baby daughter Tania lived. Her husband was killed on the front lines and Violette was shot by the Nazis. She received the George Cross medal for bravery, which was collected for her by her daughter Tania after Violette's death.

....

SONIA OLSCHANEZKY, who was born in Germany and wanted to be a dancer. Her father was a Russian Jew so Sonia was imprisoned in France for being Jewish. Her mother managed to fake some documents, which said that Sonia was needed for the German war effort. Sonia was released and continued her real work spying for the French Resistance. She was eventually captured and sent to Germany where she died with Vera Leigh.

THE WOMEN OF BLETCHLEY

Imagine completing a crossword in *The Times* newspaper and being told you had qualified as a codebreaker. That's what happened to some of the women who were recruited to the top secret codebreaking centre at Bletchley Park, a stately home in a small village in England, to help decipher secret messages during the Second World War. Two-thirds of the workforce there were women, and although a lot of them did administrative tasks, they were also involved in crucial codebreaking work and operating the vast room-sized computers. Employees had to call it 'X Station' and sign the Official Secrets Act, meaning they were not allowed to tell anyone what they did, even their families. After the war, the Bletchley workers continued to stay silent. It was only years later that the full story came out:

> *they had saved thousands of lives and shortened the war by as much as two years.*

If you were working at Bletchley you would be 'billeted' (given a place to live) in the village and at nearby RAF (Royal Air Force) centres. You would cycle or take the train to work and work in shifts: 8am to 4pm, 4pm to midnight, or midnight to 8am. Of course this could change in emergencies. Working in one of many small huts, you might spend your shift doing problem-solving and calculation tasks or translating vital messages from code. For security reasons you would never know what was going on in the other huts, only your own. Between shifts you might rehearse with the drama society, play badminton, visit the library, attend a dance or concert, go for a walk with the rambling club or relax in the clubroom.

You would need to have paid your subscription and be carrying your Bletchley Park Recreational Club card, of course. The one thing you would never do was discuss your work with anyone else.

Giant computers called Colossus were created to crack the code that Hitler used to communicate with his generals. The ten huge machines at Bletchley Park filled rooms and were the first electronic programmable computers. They needed to be running 24 hours a day so were operated on shifts by 250 members of the Woman's Royal Naval Service, nicknamed Wrens.

The Bombe was another machine that was operated by Wrens. Designed by Alan Turing, these cracked the code produced by the German Enigma machines. Operating these was hard work, dull and repetitive, but the women knew that they were doing something very important.

> *'The geese who laid the golden eggs and never cackled.'*

British Prime Minister Winston Churchill's description of the Bletchley Park codebreakers

PERSECUTION

During the Second World War, Jewish people in Germany and German-occupied countries were persecuted by the Nazi regime under Adolf Hitler, who blamed them for the problems in the country. First they were forced to wear a Star of David to show everyone they were Jewish. Then they were banned from public places and activities. Finally they were transported to concentration camps where millions died.

ANNE FRANK was a young German-Jewish girl who was delighted to receive a diary for her thirteenth birthday. Her family had already moved to the Netherlands to escape from the Nazis, but when Germany invaded, they went into hiding. They shared a cramped annex in a building with four other people. Friends brought them food as they couldn't go outside and they lived in constant fear of discovery. Anne wrote about everything in her diary, including her hopes and dreams for the future. She wanted to be a writer and worked on short stories and a novel. After two years Anne's diary came to a sudden halt.

Someone had betrayed them.

The family was captured and taken to a concentration camp. Anne, her elder sister Margot and her mother all died. Anne was a talented writer and her story brings alive the terrors of that time, helping many people today to understand what it was like. Her hiding place in Amsterdam is a museum you can visit and her diary is read by people all over the world.

MIEP GIES was an Austrian woman who worked for Anne's father's company. For two years she brought food and books to the secret annex to help her friends. She and her husband also hid a Jewish man in their own home. Miep found Anne's papers after the family were taken. She kept them safe until after the war. Without Miep, the diary would not be here today.

A FALSE EXECUTION

When Poland was occupied by Germany, Jewish people were forced to live in ghettos: crowded living areas with conditions so bad that people were dying. **IRENA SENDLER**, a Polish social worker, used her contacts to smuggle people out. If the children were orphans, she also found homes for them. Irena was captured and sentenced to death, but her colleagues managed to bribe the prison guards. When she was released, she had the strange experience of seeing posters stuck up saying she had been executed.

THE 'PERFECT' HOUSEWIFE

Even though the Second World War was over, conflict was never far away for Eve's descendants. The 1950s began violently with war in Korea and a battle over the Suez Canal in Egypt, while in Cuba there was civil war for much of the 1950s. Eve's children began to look up to the stars and wonder how to get there. 1957 saw the first satellite (a human-made object orbiting Earth) launched into space. *Sputnik 1* was the beginning of the 'space race' as the Soviet Union and America fought to exceed each other and be the first country in space.

In the fifties, women were encouraged to stick to nursing, teaching or secretarial jobs. As soon you were married, you were expected to give up your job to devote yourself to your husband, home and family. If you stayed single you could work for longer but would be an 'old maid' or 'spinster'. But the decade was bringing a change. Recovery after the war meant workers were sorely needed, and by the end of the fifties more women felt able to return to work after having their families. But your old job wouldn't be held for you. You would probably have to accept a lower-paid part-time job instead.

The perfect 1950s housewife, cheerful and energetic with her pinafore and rolling pin at the ready, was seen as something a woman should aspire to be. Pressure was on to be the perfect homemaker and, just like in the 17th century, there was plenty of advice...

ADVICE FROM 'THE GOOD WIFE'S GUIDE' IN *HOUSEKEEPING MONTHLY*:

Have a delicious meal ready for your husband when he returns home from work – he'll be hungry!

Have a tidy-up and dust before he arrives.

Don't forget yourself! Touch up your makeup and make yourself look nice for him.

Keep him entertained with interesting talk but remember, his opinions are more important than yours.

Tidy up the children and keep them quiet so he can relax.

Never complain to him – he's had a hard day.

Many housewives were unhappy and frustrated, and their feelings were captured in a book by American author **BETTY FRIEDAN**. *The Feminine Mystique*, published in the early 1960s, helped promote gender equality.

THE FEMININE MYSTIQUE

THE CIVIL RIGHTS MOVEMENT

While female stereotypes in the fifties and sixties were being challenged, the civil rights movement in America was growing. This was a protest movement to end discrimination against African-Americans. Slavery had been abolished after the American Civil War but in the southern states there were still racist laws and regulations that kept Black people out of white neighbourhoods and public areas, or forced them to use special 'coloured' areas in buses, theatres, restaurants, hospitals and schools. This was known as 'segregation'.

Women were key figures in the civil rights movement, and sometimes just a simple action can have a huge effect. That was the case for **ROSA PARKS**, an activist and member of the NAACP (National Association for the Advancement of Coloured People). In 1955 she took an ordinary bus journey in her hometown of Montgomery, Alabama, sitting in the only part she was allowed to: the 'coloured' section. The bus driver moved the sign to make the 'coloured' section even smaller so more white people could sit down. Rosa had had enough. She refused to budge. She was arrested for this, and the result was a boycott of the bus system with Black passengers refusing to travel on it. This kickstarted the newly energized civil rights movement in America.

However, not all activists were adults. **BARBARA JOHNS** was only 16 when she decided to organize a walk-out at her all-Black high school. The students were fed up with the overcrowding, poor facilities and limited subjects. Some classes even took place on school buses because there weren't enough classrooms. They wanted a new, proper school like the one the white pupils went to. Barbara and the students announced they were on strike and left. With legal help, the students then campaigned for a desegregated school with better facilities. Their case eventually helped change the law. When she grew up, Barbara became another sort of hero – a school librarian!

SEPTIMA CLARK also worked in a school. Black teachers were only allowed to work in rural schools, but Septima helped campaign for them to work in the public school system as well, and eventually succeeded. But when the school board found out she was a member of the NAACP like Rosa Parks, they fired her, even though she had protested and campaigned peacefully. Septima decided to devote all her time to activism in education. At the time, adults who couldn't pass a literacy test weren't allowed to vote, so Septima worked to improve reading and writing skills for adults. Her dream of 'citizen education' became a huge part of the civil rights movement. Separate education for Black children was banned in 1954, but it was another ten years before the Civil Rights Act was passed against discrimination.

HENRIETTA LACKS was a mother of five being treated for cervical cancer in Johns Hopkins Hospital, Baltimore, in 1951. During her treatment, some of her cells were taken to be tested in a laboratory. Sadly, Henrietta died but the HeLa cells, as they were called, were kept and used by scientists to help develop fertility treatments and the polio vaccine. Her family only found out years later that Henrietta's cells had been used without asking or even telling her about them. Henrietta is celebrated today for her contribution to medicine but also to remind us of the need for consent, respect and equal treatment for all patients.

EMPOWERED VOICES

The sixties also brought with them an era of protests, 'counterculture', assassinations and the Vietnam war. The decade was known as the 'Swinging Sixties' because of the rise of pop music and a newly empowered section of society creating their own culture and identities: teenagers!

The world began to open up to this 'in between' age group, allowing them more freedom to make decisions about their own lives and interests than they had ever had before. They were no longer just young adults or older kids and there were now products – especially fashions – aimed directly at them.

The sixties also offered new opportunities and freedoms to women. They had more control over their own choices and could plan when to start a family and had more options for their careers. This led to a second wave of feminism where newly empowered women demanded equal rights to men in more areas of life.

Unlike their suffragette predecessors, women in the 1960s fought for more than their own right to vote. They fought and protested for others around the world, becoming aware of the limitations on other people's freedoms rather than just their own. The idea that no one would really be free until everyone was free was not a new one, but it was taken up enthusiastically in this new era of Eves.

THE BIRTH OF ENVIRONMENTALISM

In 1962, American biologist **RACHEL CARSON** published a book called *Silent Spring* about the danger of pesticides. It was the first time anyone had raised concerns about chemicals like DDT used in farming and in the home. Despite being terminally ill with breast cancer, Rachel refused to give up promoting the book and her important message. 'Every once in a while in the history of mankind,' said Senator Ernest Gruening, 'a book has appeared which has substantially altered the course of history.' The pesticide DDT is now banned, but is still affecting the environment today.

THE SECOND WAVE OF FEMINISM

The vote had been won for most women, but there was still sexism in society such as women being paid lower wages, having fewer rights and being reduced to stereotypes of what people expected a woman to be. Women were still treated like second class citizens: for example, they couldn't have a credit card unless their husband allowed them to. There was also very little protection for women at work and they could be fired from their jobs for being pregnant. As well as setting up women's clinics, women during the 1960s opened the first shelters to support women who needed to leave difficult situations at home.

TECH TITANS

After hundreds of thousands of years on Earth, Eve's descendants had spread across the world, discovering remote places and amazing creatures. They had conquered mountains and explored oceans. Now they had the technology to cross the next frontier: space. And women were at the heart of that technology.

During the early days of space travel, all the calculations for the flights were done by hand. At NASA (the National Aeronautics and Space Administration), this was a team of women with pencils and paper, and they were a crucial part of getting the first American astronauts in space. The most famous are African-American mathematicians **MARY JACKSON**, **KATHERINE JOHNSON** and **DOROTHY VAUGHAN**, and there is a book and film about them. As electronic computers were gradually introduced at NASA, women were the first to use them and became pioneers in early computer programming. **MARGARET HAMILTON** developed the software for the Apollo space missions, one of which, Apollo 11, landed humans on the Moon for the very first time.

The Soviet Union had been the first to send a satellite into space. Then they sent the first man, Yuri Gagarin. Now they were the first to send a woman. **VALENTINA TERESHKOVA** was a keen skydiver who was selected for cosmonaut training by the government. Five women were trained but she was the one chosen to take a flight in the *Vostok* 6 shuttle. She spent nearly three days orbiting Earth, taking photos and recording the effects of space travel on her body. Aged 26 at the time, she is still the youngest woman to go into space and the only one to have ever flown solo. In an interview in her seventies she said she was still keen to go to Mars, even if it had to be a one-way trip!

DEFINITIONS

ASTRONAUT: an American or Western European space traveller

COSMONAUT: a Russian space traveller

TAIKONAUT: a Chinese space traveller

BYTES, BUSINESS AND BUGS

GRACE HOPPER loved finding out how things worked and explaining them to others. She found her ideal job helping to build the first computers in the navy. She played a key role in developing a language for talking to computers using words as well as numbers. This was called **COBOL**: Common Business Oriented Language. It is still used today. Grace wrote manuals, built computers and delivered hundreds of lectures, but many people remember her for coining the word 'bug' for a computer error. The reason for the strange word is that an actual moth was found in the computer!

WAR AND PEACE

The 1970s is remembered today for flamboyant fashions, big hairstyles and some pretty cool music. It was a time of peace and love, but also of anarchy and punk. Romantic relationships between people of the same sex was still illegal in most places and gay rights protestors worked to make the movement more visible. Women encouraged each other to be more empowered and to take on men at their own game – sometimes literally.

THE END OF THE VIETNAM WAR

For 21 years, North Vietnam had been at war with South Vietnam and the USA. This ended in 1975 when American troops pulled out and Vietnam became a communist regime. Women volunteers served in the US forces in supporting roles, while on the other side, Vietnamese women were crucial to the defence of supply chains, shooting down bomber planes. The women who fought directly with the National Liberation Front were known as the 'Long-Haired Army'.

BATTLE OF THE SEXES

BILLIE JEAN KING was a Grand Slam-winning female tennis player, ranked among the best in the world, so she wasn't impressed when former player Bobby Riggs suggested female players were rubbish compared to men. To prove it, he challenged her to a match. Surely even a top player like Billie Jean could not hope to beat him, a 55-year-old retired man? The televised match was the most watched of all time as Billie Jean beat Bobby with ease. Millions were inspired by her gutsy victory, and Billie Jean went on to continue to champion equality in women's sport.

FROM THE HEART

The seventies saw the rise of female singer-songwriters who sang directly about their own experiences and views. Women such as **JONI MITCHELL**, **CAROLE KING**, **JOAN ARMATRADING** and **CARLY SIMON** gave women a new, honest and relatable voice.

HELEN REDDY couldn't find a song to express how she felt about sexism in the music industry so she wrote it herself. *I am Woman* became an anthem for women's rights in the 1970s. Meanwhile **BOBBIE GENTRY** was the first female country singer to write, record, produce and perform her own material. She also designed her album covers and clothes. Bobbie left the music industry suddenly and mysteriously in 1981, to live a quiet non-celebrity life. Again, she did things on her own terms.

Near the end of the decade, an unconventional teenager called **KATE BUSH** watched a TV adaptation of Emily Brontë's *Wuthering Heights* and was fascinated by the ghost at the window. Inspired, she sat down at the piano to write a song of the same name. Kate broke records by becoming the first female to reach number one in the singles chart in the UK with a self-written song. She also shares a birthday with the author who inspired her.

AN AGE OF EXTREMES

The 1980s brought with them new technology and new extremes. Computers that had once been as big as rooms were now small enough to fit in people's homes, and children learned to code for the first time. It was also an age of inequality. Some made millions on the stock exchange while in Ethiopia over a million people died from starvation. The nuclear power plant Chernobyl in Ukraine exploded, killing around 30 people immediately and shortening the lives of thousands. The area is still uninhabitable today.

After the Second World War, Germany and its capital, Berlin, were divided between the Allies. In Berlin, a wall was put up in 1961, surrounding the western section of the city, so that no one from communist East Germany could access the west via West Germany. Even streets were divided and friends and neighbours separated. Discontent was now building up and by 1989 feelings were running high. **MARINA GRASSE** was a biologist who lived in East Berlin. She wanted to improve the city and organized a forum about education. She was expecting a few hundred people and was amazed when thousands turned up to have their say. Then people started running out. What was going on? The authorities had just announced they would be making it easier for citizens to pass through the checkpoints in the wall. People took it literally and thought they could just walk through. Thousands rushed to be reunited with their friends and family or to experience life on the other side. The situation was becoming dangerous so the barrier was opened to prevent a riot. People started chipping bits off the wall and by the end of the next month it was rubble. The fall of the wall was a huge event, reuniting Germany and symbolizing the end of the communist Soviet Union.

Before the wall came down, life for women was different on each side. In the West, you were expected to stay at home and look after the children under the guidance of your husband, while in the communist East women were expected to work and had more rights as a result, including childcare and even flexible working with an extra day off a month. However, life was harder and if you got out of line you could be spied on and reported to the terrifying Stasi (the state police) by your friends and even by your own family. After Germany was reunified, Marina Grasse created a new organization, the East-West European Women's Network, to help women from both sides understand each other's society.

Small computers had a big effect in the '80s as people went mad for computer gaming. American **CAROL SHAW** worked on games for Atari and Activision. Her most famous game was *River Raid*, a shooting game where you flew a plane over a river. The landscape moved down the screen as you flew, rather than across, which made it feel more realistic.

River Raid was so popular that Carol Shaw made lots of money from it and was able to retire early.

ROBERTA WILLIAMS is known as the queen of graphic adventure games even though she had to teach herself. She found a text adventure game she loved but when she searched for more she realized there weren't any! The only way to play was to write her own. Her husband programmed the graphics and *Mystery House* became a bestseller. The couple went on to release over 20 groundbreaking games.

BEGINNINGS AND ENDINGS

Compared to other decades, the 1990s was a little more peaceful for Eve's descendants. Apartheid – a regime of racial segregation in South Africa – came to an end and breakthroughs in computing led to an invention that would change the world forever: the internet.

Tim Berners-Lee (among others) is known as the father of the internet, but who is the mother? Some say it was American **RADIA PERLMAN**. She developed the algorithm that powers the Spanning Tree Protocol or STP, a vital part of the internet that helps computers exchange data. Radia's mother was also a computer programmer, so could she be the grandmother of the internet...?

Another important person was **ELIZABETH FEINLER**. Her sister couldn't say her name when she was a baby, so everybody called her Jake. Jake worked on the ARPANET, an early 'mini internet' used by the American military that allowed computers to talk to each other securely. She became an expert, writing manuals and running a helpline. And if you see '.com' after a website, Jake's team came up with that naming system.

THE END OF APARTHEID

Since 1948, South Africa had been controlled by the National Party, a white supremacist group who separated Black and white citizens in a system known as apartheid. The word means 'apartness', but Black South Africans were also treated very differently. They had to carry passes, which only allowed them into certain areas for work. They were exploited in mines and forced into poverty. Black South African women were an important part of the struggle against these conditions, organizing protests and leading boycotts such as refusing to use the bus service, or refusing to carry passes. Protesting was dangerous: you could be arrested or even killed. Women formed federations and movements that were continually closed down by the government, but they refused to give up.

The protests by women, men and even children were noticed by countries across the world. Some countries began sanctions against South Africa, refusing to trade with them. The pressure was on for South Africa to release their political prisoners. One man, a leading activist, had been imprisoned for 27 years. His name was Nelson Mandela and in 1990 he was finally released. Four years later he was elected president and apartheid was finally over.

ANNIE SILINGA'S GRAVE

Activist **ANNIE SILINGA** fought for the right not to be forced to carry a pass. She wouldn't give up and even went to jail a few times, once with her tiny baby. After her death, her family wanted her message to continue. They asked for a special inscription to be placed at her grave. It read:

'I will never carry a pass.'

NEW MILLENNIUM, NEW CHALLENGES

In 1999 people around the world were terrified – of the date changing! The fear was that when the year ticked over from 1999 to 2000 it would bring down computer systems and cause chaos. Luckily with a few programming changes everything was fine, but other world events were a lot more serious. Terrorist attacks like the one on the World Trade Center in New York in 2001 (known as 9/11 after the date it happened) rocked the world, leading to wars in Afghanistan and Iraq. A financial crisis in 2008 caused a new worldwide recession, where growth slows and unemployment increases. And there were huge natural disasters such as the massive tsunami in the Indian Ocean where an underwater earthquake caused giant waves in 2004, killing 230,000 people. It was also the decade when social media, reality TV and digital music and books became part of our lives.

Plenty of people know about Mark Zuckerberg starting Facebook in 2004, but did you know about **STACY HORN** and ECHO? Stacy had already predicted that social networking or 'computer conferencing', as she called it, was going to be the next big thing. She tried a networking group at her workplace, but it wasn't supported.

But Stacy had a hunch.

When she left that workplace in 1989 she decided to create her own social network in New York, which she called the East Coast Hangout or ECHO. Investors told her the idea would only appeal to weirdos, so Stacy used her own money and her own small apartment.

Her hunch wasn't wrong. ECHO got so popular her apartment block had to install special cabling for her, and the internet modem, which helped adapt the digital information to go down the phone lines, heated up the whole room. ECHO didn't become as successful as Facebook, but Stacey's network inspired users to start new businesses, form new relationships, and even create their own social networks such as BlackPlanet – all from one small apartment room.

The 2000s also saw many countries electing women as their presidents and prime ministers. India, Finland, Ireland, Latvia, Chile, Moldova, Iceland, Lithuania, the Philippines, Ukraine, Senegal, Indonesia, Liberia, Jamaica and Croatia all had female leaders at some point during the 2000s. Perhaps the most successful was **ANGELA MERKEL**, chancellor of Germany from 2005 to 2021. At one time considered to be the most powerful woman in the world, Angela is also a doctor of quantum chemistry!

PROTESTS AND THE PLANET

During the 2010s, the number of Eve's descendants passed seven billion, and they were now having a huge impact on plants, animals and the environment. Scientists warned of disaster if humans did not change the way they used the world's resources. The internet and social media meant people across the world could see and follow protestors such as the teenager Greta Thunberg, and movements such as Black Lives Matter and Me Too took off globally thanks to women taking a stand.

In 2013, three women started using the hashtag #Blacklivesmatter on their social media after a tragic event. An unarmed Black teenage boy, Trayvon Martin, had been shot dead in 2012 by a man on neighbourhood watch duty. Trayvon was just visiting his father, but the man, who was on the lookout for burglars, decided he was acting suspiciously. Police let the man go and it was only after a petition by Trayvon's father, supported by the public, that the case went to court. Even then, the jury decided he could go free. The three woman – **ALICIA GARZA**, **PATRISSE KHAN-CULLORS** and **OPAL TOMETI** – were outraged. They founded the Black Lives Matter organization to highlight racism and protest against violence towards Black people and communities.

The Me Too movement reached millions of people in 2017 when a Hollywood actress used the phrase as a hashtag to draw attention to the treatment of women in the film industry. In fact, **TARANA BURKE** had started the Me Too organization over a decade before in 2006 to help survivors of sexual violence, particularly girls and women of colour. The hashtag helped to spread the message and empower women to speak up. Tarana continues to offer support programmes and raise awareness around the world. She has also written a book about how her own difficult experiences inspired her to help others.

How much can one teenager do to save the planet? A whole lot, that's how much!

Swedish teenager **GRETA THUNBERG** was just 15 when she led a protest outside parliament in 2018 for more to be done about climate change. She began 'going on strike' from school every Friday and encouraged other children to do the same at their own schools. Two months later, 24 countries were taking part. By the next year, Greta had become a famous speaker and was named one of the most influential people in the world. She even made a speech to world leaders at the United Nations summit.

Greta showed not only that action needs to be taken to protect the world, but that one girl can make a world of difference.

SPRINTING AHEAD

Life is still not easy for Eve and her family. In 2020 a new virus swept the world. COVID – short for Coronavirus Disease – began in China and spread rapidly, going on to kill millions and affecting everybody's lives and jobs through lockdowns and restrictions. Meanwhile bushfires destroyed many animal habitats in Australia. And in the same decade, new wars in Ukraine and Western Asia shocked the world.

The year 2023 was record-breaking for women's sport, as it finally began to get the attention it deserves. Football fever took over as more than 21 million people around the world watched Spain beat England to win the Women's World Cup Football final. And three million watched American teenager **COCO GAUFF** win the US Open tennis championship. Coco's match was played on the same day that Billie Jean King beat Bobby Riggs in the Battle of the Sexes in 1973, and Billie Jean presented Coco with her trophy!

2023 also saw the largest live attendance for a women's sporting event ever – between two universities. Over 92,000 fans crammed into the Memorial stadium in Nebraska USA to watch the volleyball match between Nebraska and Omaha (Nebraska won 3–0).

Women are still paid less, on average, than men, and in women's sports the difference can be huge. Women sometimes receive less than half the prize money men get for the same sport. One of the most equally paid sports is probably tennis, thanks to Billie Jean King fighting for equal pay in the US Open championships. But it hasn't happened for all sports. Equal pay is another challenge female sportswomen have to overcome.

WOMEN SMASHING RECORDS

Women are still breaking sporting records. Here are a few that were broken in 2023:

SIMONE BILES from the USA became the woman who had won the most medals ever in gymnastics, including seven Olympic medals.

TIGST ASSEFA from Ethiopia ran the fastest ever women's marathon time. It took her just 2 hours, 11 minutes and 53 seconds to run the 26 gruelling miles. Before 1972, women were seen as too weak and feminine to be allowed to compete in marathons.

KRISTIN HARILA, a skier from Norway, completed the fastest climb of the 14 highest mountains in the world. With a support team and climbing partner, she took three months and one day to do the lot.

Kenyan **FAITH KIPYEGON** broke the world record for the fastest ever women's mile: 4 minutes and 7.64 seconds. Super-talented Faith also holds the record for the fastest women's 1,500 metres, which she set in 2024. Her sporting nickname is 'the smiling destroyer'!

KARIN SINNIGER, a Swiss lawyer living in Texas, USA, broke the record for scuba diving in the most countries: 180! Karin hasn't relaxed though – she's still looking for new and exciting places to dive.

EVE'S LEGACY

There are more than four billion women and girls in the world. All humans have mitochondrial DNA passed down from mother to daughter from just one woman. We are all related. We are family. And we have a lot to be proud of. Women have climbed Everest, gone into space, sailed round the world, made amazing discoveries and inventions, created life-changing art and, most importantly, helped each other be the best people possible. The *Shevolution* is unstoppable! But there is still more to be done to help women, and particularly girls, live their best lives around the world.

In most of the nations around the world, the youngest age you can marry is 18. But in some countries, girls are forced into early marriages, missing out on school, becoming very young mothers and taking on a role they aren't ready for. There are many campaigns around the world to help make sure that girls can wait and decide for themselves when, or if, they marry.

Many women and girls don't have access to sanitary pads or tampons when they have their period, or can't afford them. Sometimes they are made to feel ashamed or unclean. Campaigners are working to improve this. In some places period products are supplied for free, and Scotland is the first country in the world to make period products free to all.

All children should have the same right to an education, but in reality, this isn't always the case. Girls in poorer parts of the world can miss out on school due to early marriage, having their period or being kept at home to do chores. In countries suffering disasters or war, the situation is even worse.

MALALA TAKES A STAND

MALALA YOUSAFZAI was born in Pakistan in 1997, and enjoyed school until her area was taken over by the Taliban. Their strict regime meant no music and television, and girls weren't allowed to go to school. Malala didn't think that was right and made her feelings known. One day a gunman boarded the bus she was on, asked which one was Malala and shot her in the head. She was taken to the UK for treatment. Amazingly, Malala survived. Even more amazingly, she decided to devote her life to helping girls get the education they need. She started her own charity and travels the world inspiring people. In 2014 her work won her the Nobel Peace Prize. At just 17 she was the youngest winner ever.

WHAT'S NEXT?

You have mitochondrial DNA inside you, passed down from our common female ancestor, Eve. Everyone is part of the *Shevolution*. Women throughout time have had to struggle to be heard, to make their way in a society stacked against them, and to be their full and amazing selves. But they have also achieved incredible things.

We've lived through thousands of years of history, from the Stone Age to the ancient world to the darkest of times and on to incredible changes. We've travelled from southern Africa to the empires of Western Asia, Europe and Japan, and met women and girls from in every time and every place. We've experienced incredible leaps in technology and great societal change. And we've learned that every person on this planet is important, and so are you.

You are a part of the power of the Shevolution.

GLOSSARY

Ancestors – the family members that produced you: your parents, grandparents, great-grandparents and so on

Anthology – a collection of writings

Assassination – a planned killing by surprise attack, usually for political reasons

BCE – Before the Common Era, up to the year 1 BCE. The years count backwards, so a bigger date is longer ago.

Calligrapher – someone who practises the art of beautiful writing

CE – Common Era, from the year 1 CE onwards

Celtic – relating to the Celts, a people of ancient Britain, Ireland and northern France

Civil rights – the right for all people to be equal members of society

Codebreaking – figuring out how a code works in order to translate encoded messages

Communism – a system of governing with the aim that everyone contributes and benefits equally

Concentration camp – an inhumane way of interring prisoners of war and persecuted minorities

Convention – a large public meeting to explore ideas or topics

Corset – a restrictive undergarment designed to pull in the waist

Democracy – a system of governing by elected representatives based on the will of the majority

Descendants – the family members that you produce that will come after you: your children, your grandchildren and so on

Dictatorship – rule by one leader who has absolute power

Enlist – to join something, particularly the armed forces

Feudal – a class system with serfs at the bottom and the king or queen at the top

Forum – a meeting for discussion

Fossil – the imprint of a plant or creature preserved in rock

Great Britain – the countries of Scotland, England and Wales

Guillotine – a device for executing people, used particularly in Revolutionary France

Indigenous – the original inhabitants of a land

Merchant – someone who trades

Mesopotamia – an ancient region of Western Asia

Munitions – military weapons and equipment

Ninja – a skilled Japanese spy trained in stealth and warfare

Nobel Prize – an international award given each year to people outstanding in the fields of physics, chemistry, medicine, literature, economic sciences and peace

Nun – a woman who devotes herself to her religion, often living separately from the world

Observatory – a place with equipment and views of the sky built to study the stars

Oracle – someone who predicts the future

Pagan – someone with ancient beliefs that aren't part of an organized religion

Peasant – someone from the poorest section of a society

Persia – a historic region of Western Asia, now mainly Iran

Pesticide – a chemical used to kill pests such as insects on crops

Petition – a document demanding change, signed by several people, which is presented to the authorities

Pharaoh – an ancient Egyptian king

Priestess – a woman who serves a god or goddess

Reform – the act of working to change something for the better

Revolution – an oppressed section of society turning on their oppressors

Sacrifice – in religion, an animal or human killed (sometimes symbolically) to please the gods

Samurai – the ancient warrior class of Japan

Scribe – in ancient times, a writer, someone who kept written records

Spinster – the old fashioned term for an older single woman, from the job of spinning wool

Star of David – a symbol of the Jewish religion

Suffrage – the right to vote

Suffragette – a member of a women's organization in the early 20th century who fought for the right to vote in public elections in the United Kingdom

Taliban – an Islamic militant faction with strict religious views

Terrorist – a person who uses surprise violent attacks against civilians for a political cause

UK – the United Kingdom: Scotland, England, Wales and Northern Ireland

USA or US – the United States of America

Western Asia – the area that includes countries such as Iran, Iraq, Saudi Arabia, Egypt and Turkey, also known as the Middle East

White House – the official residence of the President of the United States of America

INDEX

Agnodice (doctor) 13
Agojie (Dahomey warriors) 42
Agrippina the Elder (Roman) 18
Agrippina the Younger (Roman) 18
Aitken, Margaret ('Great Witch') 32
Anguissola, Sofonisba (artist) 29
Anning, Mary (palaeontologist) 44–5
Arzner, Dorothy (film director) 62
Assefa, Tigst (athlete) 91
Ayrton, Hertha (scientist) 56

Biles, Simone (gymnast) 91
Borgia, Lucrezia (noblewoman) 28
Brontë sisters (authors) 51
Burke, Tarana (activist) 88
Bush, Kate (singer-songwriter) 80

Carson, Rachel (biologist and writer) 77
Cavell, Edith (nurse) 60
Chisholm, Mairi (nurse and ambulance driver) 60
Christine de Pizan (writer) 20
Clark, Septima (activist) 74
Coleman, Bessie (pilot) 64
Corday, Charlotte (revolutionary) 38
Curie, Marie (scientist) 56

Davison, Emily (suffragette) 54
Distaff Gospels (wise women) 24–5

Earhart, Amelia (pilot) 64–5
Eleanor of Aquitaine (Queen of France and England) 23
Elizabeth I (Queen of England and Ireland) 34
Elizabeth II (Queen of the United Kingdom and other Commonwealth realms) 66
Enheduanna (priestess) 11
Este, Isabella d' (patron) 28–9
Eve, mitochondrial (most recent common ancestor) 6–7

Feinler, Elizabeth (information scientist) 84
Frank, Anne (writer) 71

Gauff, Coco (tennis player) 90
Gentry, Bobby (singer-songwriter) 80
Gies, Miep (Righteous Among the Nations, non-Jews who risked their lives to save Jews) 71
goddesses 10–11, 13, 15
Gouges, Olympe de (playwright) 38
Grasse, Marina (biologist) 82

Hamilton, Margaret (computer scientist) 78
Harila, Kristin (skier) 91
Hatshepsut (Queen of Egypt) 13
Hildegard of Bingen (nun) 23
Hollenstein, Stephanie (artist) 58
Hopper, Grace (computer scientist) 78
Horn, Stacy (businesswoman) 87
Huldremose Woman (bog body) 14
Hurston, Zora Neale (writer and anthropologist) 65

Inglis, Elsie (doctor) 59
Irdabama (merchant) 16
Izumi Shikibu (poet) 26

Jex-Blake, Sophia (teacher and physician) 44
Johns, Barbara (activist) 74
Johnson, Amy (pilot) 65
Johnson, Elizabeth, Jr ('witch') 32
Julia the Elder (Roman) 18

Khan, Noor Inayat (resistance agent) 66
King, Billie Jean (tennis player) 80, 90
Knocker, Elsie (nurse and ambulance driver) 60
Kuroda, Chika (scientist) 57

Lacks, Henrietta (cancer patient) 74
Lagerlöf, Selma (author) 54
Leigh, Vera (spy) 66

Mbande, Njinga (Queen of Mbundo people) 34
Meitner, Lise (scientist) 57

Nawi (warrior) 42

Olschanezky, Sonia (spy) 66
Oracle (priestess) 16–17

Parks, Rosa (activist) 74
Paul, Alice (suffragette) 54
Payne-Gaposchkin, Cecilia (astronomer) 57
Perlman, Radia (computer programmer) 84
Pickford, Mary (actress and producer) 62

Reddy, Helen (singer-songwriter) 80
Roosevelt, Eleanor ('First Lady') 64

Savs, Viktoria (soldier) 58
Sendler, Irena (social worker) 71
Shaw, Carol (game designer) 82
Sheppard, Kate (activist) 52
Shilling, Beatrice (engineer) 6
Shin Saimdang (artist and poet) 37
Silinga, Annie (activist) 84
Smirnow, Zoya (soldier) 58
Stanton, Elizabeth Cady (activist) 52
Szabo, Violette (spy) 66

Tereshkova, Valentina (cosmonaut) 78
Thunberg, Greta (activist) 88
Tomoe Gozen (samurai) 26
Truth, Sojourner (activist) 48
Tubman, Harriet (activist) 48

Victoria (Queen of Great Britain and Ireland, and the British Empire) 46

Williams, Roberta (game designer) 83

Yousafzai, Malala (activist) 92